American Favorite Ballads

Tunes and Songs as Sung by

Pete Seeger

Oak Publications
New York / London / Sydney / Cologne

Edited for publication by Irwin Silber and Ethel Raim
Editorial Assistant: Daryl Heymann
Music transcribed and edited by Ethel Raim
Illustrations selected by and from the collection of Moses Asch
Additional illustrations from the New York Public Library and The
Library of Congress.

Other books by Peter Seeger:

How To Play The 5-String Banjo
The Steel Drums of Kim Loy Wong
The 12-String Guitar as Played by Leadbelly
Bells of Rhymney
Bits and Pieces
Oh Had I A Golden Thread

International Standard Book Number: 0.8256.0028.6
Library of Congress Catalog Card Number: M61-1008

Exclusive Distributors:
Music Sales Corporation
24 East 22nd Street, New York, NY 10010 USA
Music Sales Limited
8/9 Frith Street, London W1V 5TZ England
Music Sales Pty. Limited
120 Rothschild Street, Rosebery, Sydney, NSW 2018, Australia

Printed in the United States of America by
Vicks Lithograph and Printing Corporation

Contents

Acknowledgements and Sources

I must accept responsibility for the versions of the songs printed in this book. After singing a song for many years, one finds somehow it has changed. I hope that those who learn from this book will similarly make the songs their own. Here we would like to credit the authors, the folk song collectors, the folksingers, and the books in which the songs were first printed, as accurately as we can ascertain.   (P. S.)

The following songs are printed by permission:

Alabama Bound - from the singing of Huddie Ledbetter; also from "American Ballads and Folksongs" by John A. and Alan Lomax.

Buffalo Skinners - traditional as adapted by Woody Guthrie; copyright 1961 by Fall River Music Inc.

Come All You Fair and Tender Ladies - collected by Cecil Sharpe; copyright Novello and Co., Ltd.

Devilish Mary - from "Our Singing Country" by John A. and Alan Lomax.

Dink's Song - from "American Ballads and Folksongs" by John A. and Alan Lomax.

Erie Canal - from "American Ballads and Folksongs" by John A. and Alan Lomax.

Fillimeeooreay - from "Our Singing Country" by John A. and Alan Lomax.

Four Nights Drunk - traditional, except for third verse by Pete Seeger.

The Hammer Song - words and music by Lee Hays and Pete Seeger; copyright 1958 by Ludlow Music Inc.

Hard Traveling - words and music by Woody Guthrie; copyright 1959 by Ludlow Music Inc.

House of the Rising Sun - from "Our Singing Country" by John A. and Alan Lomax; from the singing of Georgia Turner and Bert Morton.

I Never Will Marry - words and music adapted and arranged by Mrs. Texas Gladden, copyright 1958 by Melody Trails, Inc.

Irene Goodnight - from the singing of Huddie Ledbetter and from "Negro Folk Songs as Sung by Leadbelly" by John A. and Alan Lomax.

Kisses Sweeter Than Wine - words by Paul Campbell (The Weavers); music by Joel Newman (Huddie Ledbetter); copyright 1951 by Folkways Music Inc.

Little Girl - from the singing of Huddie Ledbetter. (FA 2014)

Michael, Row The Boat Ashore - traditional Afro-American song learned from Tony Saletan; copyright 1958 by Sanga Music Inc.

Midnight Special - from "Our Singing Country" by John A. and Alan Lomax; and from the singing of Huddie Ledbetter.

Passing Through - words by Dick Blakeslee; tune adapted from a gospel hymn; copyright 1948 by Dick Blakeslee.

Pick A Bale of Cotton - from "Negro Folk Songs As Sung By Leadbelly" by John A. and Alan Lomax.

Putting On The Style - from the singing of Ernie Sager and Camp Woodland campers; collected by Norman Cazden.

Que Bonita Bandera - Author Unknown

Reuben James - words by (and music adapted by) Woody Guthrie and The Almanac Singers; copyright by Leeds Music Inc.

Rye Whiskey - from "Cowboy Songs" by John A. Lomax.

So Long, It's Been Good To Know You - words by (and music adapted by) Woody Guthrie; copyright 1950 and 1951 by Folkways Music Inc.

Strangest Dream - words and music by Ed McCurdy, copyright 1950 by Folkways Music Inc.

Streets of Laredo - from "Cowboy Songs" by John A. Lomax

This Land Is Your Land - words and music by Woody Guthrie; copyright 1956 and 1958 by Ludlow Music Inc.

Twelve Gates To The City - adapted by Marion Hicks; copyright 1961 by Stormking Music Inc.

The Water Is Wide - from "English Folksongs from the Southern Appalachians" by Cecil Sharpe; copyright by Novello and Co. Ltd., 1908 and 1936.

When I First Came To This Land - English lyrics by Oscar Brand; music traditional; from "Singing Holidays" by Oscar Brand, copyright 1957.

Which Side Are You On? - words by Florence Reece, music traditional; copyright by Sing Out Inc.

Who's Gonna Shoe Your Pretty Little Foot? - adapted by Woody Guthrie, copyright 1961 by Stormking Music Inc.

The following songs are to the best of our knowledge, in the public domain, therefore no permission is necessary to reprint the versions given in this book.

Aunt Rhody - words: traditional; tune first printed by John Jacques Rousseau (1752)

Barbara Allen - traditional

Big Rock Candy Mountain - adapted originally by Mac McClintock

Blow the Man Down - traditional

Blue-Tail Fly - from the original song by Daniel Emmett. Folk Version collected by Dorothy Scarborough.

Buffalo Gals - traditional

Camptown Races - words and music by Stephen Foster

Careless Love - traditional

Cielito Lindo - Author Unknown

Cindy - traditional

Clementine - Author Unknown

Crawdad - traditional

Cumberland Gap - traditional

Darling Corey - traditional from Aunt Molly Jackson, B. F. Shelton, others

Deep Blue Sea - traditional

Devil and the Farmer's Wife - traditional

Down in the Valley - traditional

The Farmer Is The Man - Author Unknown

The Fox - traditional

Frankie and Johnny - traditional

Froggie Went A-Courtin' - traditional

Hold The Fort - melody by P. P. Bliss, 1870; author of words unknown (circa 1880 - 1890)

Home on the Range - traditional from the collection of John A. Lomax

I Ride An Old Paint - traditional from the collection of Margaret Larkin

Jesse James - traditional

Joe Bowers - Author Unknown

John Brown's Body - traditional; one verse here from "Battle Hymn of the Republic" by Julia Ward Howe

John Henry - traditional

Joshua Fought the Battle of Jericho - traditional

The Keeper - traditional

My Horses Ain't Hungry - traditional

New River Train - traditional

Oh Mary Don't You Weep - traditional

Oh Susanna - words and music by Stephen Foster

Old Dan Tucker - from the original song by Daniel Emmett

Old Joe Clark - traditional

On Top of Old Smoky - traditional

Riddle Song - traditional

Sally Ann - traditional

Shenandoah - traditional

Skip To My Lou - traditional

Solidarity Forever - words by Ralph Chaplin; music: "John Brown's Body"

Sometimes I Feel Like A Motherless Child - traditional

Stagolee - traditional

Study War No More - traditional

Swanee River - words and music by Stephen Foster

Swing Low, Sweet Chariot - traditional

Wabash Cannonball - Author Unknown

Wayfaring Stranger - traditional

We Shall Not Be Moved - traditional

Yankee Doodle - traditional

Young Man Who Wouldn't Hoe Corn - traditional; from Resettlement Administration Songsheet, 1935

Foreword

This land is your land,
This land is my land,
From California to the New York Island,
From the Redwood Forest to the Gulf Stream waters. . .*

The ever-continuing search of Americans for an identity of belonging is best exemplified through our folk music — in song, ballad and tune. As Woody Guthrie pointed out in the song quoted above — this is a big country. People from all walks of life and areas of the world have made America their home. Their children and grandchildren have left behind most of the ethnic ties that bound the old folks to their previous homelands. The schools, newspapers, novels, and media of the airwaves keep reminding them of the history that made the United States the land they know today.

This history is filled with the heartaches, hardships, triumphs, disasters and love that have molded us all into a common experience. It is these qualities which folk music reflects — from "Yankee Doodle" of the Revolution to the desires for a better world expressed in "Passing Through." Appropriately enough, both of these songs are in this collection.

It was not until after World War II that young people in all walks of life and all parts of the United States made use of this folk music tradition and adapted it to their way of expressing their feelings and of tying up the past to their future.

Pete Seeger, of all the singers of folk song, made the transition possible for them. In the past 15 years, Pete Seeger's concerts — from Carnegie Hall in New York to the smallest school auditorium in the hinterlands — have helped to spread the folk music seed. And, in the tradition of Johnny Appleseed, what Pete Seeger has sown over these years, has grown, until now the tree is ripe and one can issue a book such as this without fear of contradiction or a patronizing pat on the back — for the song has come from the earth, regrown, and attained maturity.

Now it is up to the children and grandchildren to take it from here. Folkways Records, Pete Seeger, Sing Out magazine, and the host of folk song collectors, folk singers and record companies have made their contribution.

And so this volume is dedicated to the young. But in making such a dedication, the others should not be forgotten. As Woody Guthrie advised those who heard and sang his "Songs To Grow On":

"Now I don't want to see you use these songs to divide nor split your family all apart. I mean, don't just buy this book and take it home and keep it to yourself. Get your whole family into the fun. Get papa. Get mama. Get brother. Get sister. Get aunty. . . The friends. The neighbors. Everybody."

— Moses Asch

* — As Woody Guthrie recorded this during the original session for Moses Asch.

JOHNNY APPLESEED

Introduction

This book is dedicated with thanks, to many people:

The song makers, long dead and nameless;
The joky boys, the singing grandparents, the fun-lovers,
    who carried the songs along;
The serious collectors and librarians who copied them down
    for us;
The inkstained printers and the chemical papermakers and
    the inventors of their machines, who made us this book;
And the desk girls and countermen who saw it to our hands;
Let us thank them all, and be glad, too, that we are part of
    the chain.

Now, if you love one of these songs, you can make it your own by singing it; through the years it will become part of your life as little by little you change the tune in subtle ways, or add or subtract verses. This is what I have done. As a matter of fact, without a certain amount of creative rearranging some of the songs in this book will be impossible to sing. For example, you will probably have to adjust the pitch of many songs to fit the range of your voice, or voices.

As for myself, I should like to specifically thank my parents for the music I got from them; Alan Lomax for first introducing me to the length and breadth of American music; Huddie Ledbetter and Woody Guthrie, two of the best musicians I've ever known, for showing me details of style that I could never learn from books or records. Lastly, Moe Asch and Irwin Silber of Folkways Records and Sing Out magazine for getting this collection out. Formal acknowledgements for copyright permissions are made on the next page. The sequence of the songs has purposely been made from a singer's or a listener's point of view, rather than for any literary or historic grouping.

A good song is like a many-faceted jewel. Or a woman of many moods. Or a tool of many uses. Try these out, turn them over, look at them from several angles. Taste 'em. On these pages they are in a state of suspended animation. It takes singers to bring them to life. And such is their magic, that they can bring fuller life to you.

Peter Seeger
Dutchess Junction
Beacon, N.Y.
Dec. 1960

Careless Love

(One of the greatest American songs — I've heard it from so many sources, I don't know where to credit it.)

Love, oh, love oh care-less love.   Love, oh, love oh care-less love   Love, oh, love, oh, care-less love, You see what love has done to me.

I love my mama and papa too,   (3)
I'd leave them both to go with you.

What, oh what, will mama say,   (3)
When she learns I've gone astray.

Once I wore my apron low,   (3)
I couldn't scarcely keep you from my
     door.

Now my apron strings don't pin,   (3)
You pass my door and you don't come
     in.

Don't you marry a railroad man (2)
A railroad man will kill you if he can,
And he'll drink your blood, drink it
     like wine.

Repeat first verse from time to time
as a chorus if you wish.

The Blue-Tail Fly

(I was on a CBS radio show in 1940 when Alan Lomax first taught this song to Burl Ives, who made it practically his theme song. Alan got it from a collection by Dorothy Scarborough, "On The Trail of Negro Folksong." It is a folk variant of a popular composed minstrel song of the 1840's. You change it some more.)

When I was young I used to wait on mas-ter and serve him his plate, And pass the bot-tle when he got dry, And brush a-way the Blue-tail Fly.

Chorus

Jim-my crack corn and I don't care. Jim-my crack corn and I don't care. Jim-my crack corn and I don't care, My mas-ter's gone a-way.

And when he'd ride in the afternoon
I'd follow with a hickory broom,
The pony being rather shy
When bitten by the Blue Tail Fly. (Cho.)

One day he rode around the farm
The flys so numerous they did swarm,
One chanced to bite him on the thigh
The devil take a Blue Tail Fly. (Cho.)

The pony jump, he toss, he pitch
He threw my master in the ditch,
He died and the jury wondered why
The verdict was the Blue Tail Fly.
(Cho.)

He lies beneath a 'simmon tree
His epitaph is there to see,
Beneath this stone I'm forced to lie
The victim of a Blue Tail Fly. (Cho.)

When I First Came To This Land

(Credit Oscar Brand with the English words to this old Pennsylvania Dutch song. Translating poetry is one of the world's most difficult, though needed, tasks. The tune, of course, is a famous melody known in every country of Europe.)

(See page 4 for acknowledgement of printed source.)

When I first came to this land, I was not a weal-thy man.

So I got my-self a
1. shack
2. cow
3. duck
I did what I could. And I called my shack

"Break my back" — But the land was sweet and good, and I did what I could.

called my cow "No milk now", And I called my shack, "Break my back"

But the land was sweet and good and I did what I could.

called my duck, "Out of luck", And I called my cow,

"No milk now," called my shack, "Break my back" But the land was

sweet and good and I did what I could.

(Add Verses 4 & 5 in a similar cumulative manner)

4th verse: wife
Called my wife, run for your life.

5th verse: son
Called my son, my work's done.

Que Bonita Bandera

(A patriotic song I learned in 1955 from young Puerto Ricans living in New York. I've been unable to locate the composer. If you cannot sing the chorus in harmony, the melody of the alto part should be sung, rather than the soprano.)

Chorus

Cm — G7

Que bo- ni- ta ban- der- a,

Cm

Que bo- ni- ta ban- der- a, Que bo- ni- ta ban-

Fm — Cm — G7 — Cm

de- ra, es la ban- der- a Puer- to- ri- que- ña.

Verse — G7 — Cm

Az- ul blan-ca y co-lo __ ra-da, G7 y en el

G7 — Cm

me-dio tiene __ un es- trel —la; Bo- ni- ta se-

Cm — Fm — Cm — G7 — Cm

ñor- es es la ban- der- a Puer- to ri- que- ña.

Todo buen Puertoriqueña,
Es bueno que la defienda,
Bonita señores, es la bandera
    Puertoriqueña.

Chorus

Bonita senora es,
Que bonita es ella,
Que bonita es la bandera
    Puertoriqueña.

Chorus

Wayfaring Stranger

(What has been called a "white spiritual," this song used to be printed in the old "shape-note" hymn books, with notes shaped in triangular, square, and diamond shapes, etc. for easier part singing.)

I'm just a poor way-far-ing strang-er, A- trav'- ling through this world of woe; But there's no sick- ness no toil nor dan-ger, in that bright world to which I go. I'm go- ing there to see my fa-ther, I'm go-ing there no more to roam, I'm just a- go- ing o-ver Jor-dan, I'm just a – go- ing o- ver home.

Swing Low, Sweet Chariot

(The genius of the unknown, unlettered folk composer confounds the literary teacher. "Chariots don't swing, they roll," a critic would have marked this poem and sent it back for revision.)

Swing low, sweet char-i-ot, Com-ing for to car-ry me home, Swing low sweet char-i-ot com-ing for to car-ry me home. I looked o-ver Jor-dan and what did I see? Com-ing for to car-ry me home. A band of an-gels com-ing af-ter me, Com-ing for to car-ry me home.

If you get there, before I do,
Tell all my friends, I'm coming too.
(Cho.)

Shenandoah

(Question: Why should this famous sea shanty concern an Indian chief, and a midwestern river? And why does everyone love it so and refuse to change it?)

Flowing

Oh, Shen-an-doah, I long to see you, a-
way you roll-ing riv-er. Oh, Shen-an-doah, I long to
see you, a-way, I'm bound a-way, 'cross the wide Mis-
sou-ri. _____ Oh, -ri.

O, Shenandoah, I love your daughter,
   Away, you rolling river —
O, Shenandoah, I love your daughter,
   Away, we're bound away, 'cross
   the wide Missouri.

O, Shenandoah, I long to see you,
   Away, you rolling river —
O, Shenandoah, I'll not deceive you,
   Away, we're bound away, 'cross
   the wide Missouri.

O, seven years, I've been a rover,
   Away, you rolling river —
For seven years I've been a rover,
   Away, we're bound away, 'cross
   the wide Missouri.

House Of The Rising Sun

(This song I first learned from Alan Lomax, though I've since heard it in other versions: major instead of minor, $\frac{4}{4}$ time instead of $\frac{3}{4}$, etc.)

(See page 4 for acknowledgement of printed source.)

There is a house in New Or - leans, They call the Ris - ing Sun.___ Has been the ru-in of ma - ny poor girls and me, Oh, Lord I'm one.___

My mother she's a tailor, she sews
    those new blue jeans,
My husband he's a gambling man,
    drinks down in New Orleans.

My husband he's a gambler, he goes
    from town to town,
The only time he's satisfied, is when
    he drinks his liquor down.

Go tell my baby sister, never do like
    I have done,
Shun that house in New Orleans, they
    call the Rising Sun.

One foot on the platform, the other's
    on the train,
I'm going down to New Orleans, to
    wear that ball and chain.

Going back to New Orleans, my race
    is almost run,
I'm going to spend the rest of my life,
    beneath that Rising Sun.

The Hammer Song

(Words by Lee Hays. Music by Pete Seeger. We wrought better than we thought. The song has grown with time.)

(See page 4 for acknowledgement of printed source.)

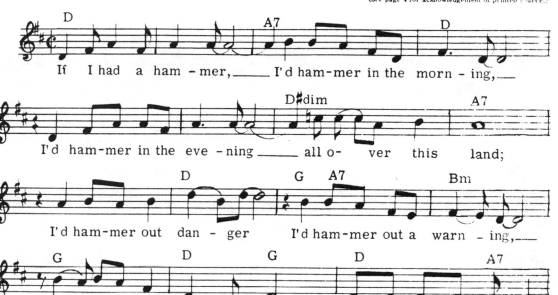

If I had a ham-mer, _____ I'd ham-mer in the morn-ing, _____ I'd ham-mer in the eve-ning _____ all o-ver this land; I'd ham-mer out dan-ger I'd ham-mer out a warn-ing, _____ I'd ham-mer out love be-tween my bro-thers and my sis-ters, All _____ o-ver this land. _____

If I had a bell, I'd ring it in the
    morning
I'd ring it in the evening all over this
    land;
I'd ring out danger, I'd ring out a
    warning
I'd ring out love between my brothers
    and my sisters
All over this land.

If I had a song, I'd sing it in the
    morning
I'd sing it in the evening all over this
    land;
I'd sing out danger, I'd sing out a
    warning
I'd sing out love between my brothers
    and my sisters
All over this land.

Well I got a hammer and I got a bell
And I got a song to sing all over this
    land;
It's the hammer of justice, it's the
    bell of freedom
It's the song about love between my
    brothers and my sisters
All over this land.

Hold The Fort

(Tune from a gospel hymn composed at the time of the Civil War. These words are generally credited to some English transport workers, on strike in the late 19th Century.)

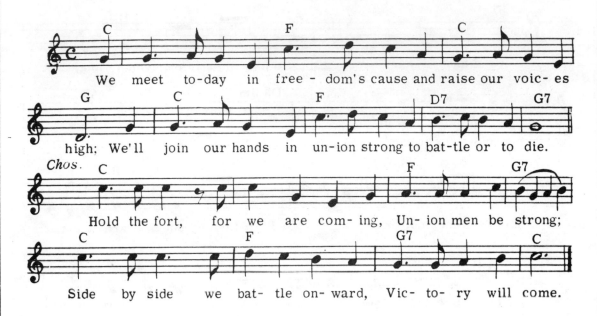

We meet to-day in free-dom's cause and raise our voic-es high; We'll join our hands in un-ion strong to bat-tle or to die.

Chos.

Hold the fort, for we are com-ing, Un-ion men be strong;

Side by side we bat-tle on-ward, Vic-to-ry will come.

Look my comrades, see the union,
Banners waving high;
Reinforcements now appearing
Victory is nigh —   (Cho.)

See our numbers still increasing,
Hear the bugles blow;
By our union we will triumph
Over every foe —   (Cho.)

THE LABOR TROUBLES OF 1877. RIOTS AT THE HALSTED STREET VIADUCT CHICAGO.

My Horses Ain't Hungry

(My father was doing some folksong research in Washington D. C. in the 1930's. I learned this then. It is one of a large family. "Rye Whisky" and "On Top of Old Smoky" are both cousins.)

My hor-ses ain't hun-gry, They won't eat your hay.____ So

fare you well Pol-ly, I'm go-ing a way. Your par-ents don't

like me, they say I'm too poor, They say I'm not wor-thy to en-ter your

door.

My parents don't like you, you're poor I am told,
But it's your love I'm wanting, not silver or gold.
Then come with me Polly, we'll ride till we come
To some little cabin, we'll call it our home.

Sparking is pleasure, but parting is grief,
And a false hearted lover is worse than a thief.
A thief will just rob you and take what you have,
But a false hearted lover will lead you to the grave.

Four Nights Drunk

Additional words by Pete Seeger, Lee Hays, Fred Hellerman & Ronnie Gilbert. © Copyright 1958 by SANGA MUSIC INC. All Rights Reserved. Used by Permission.

(He) I came home the oth-er night as drunk as I could be, I saw a horse in the sta-ble where my horse ought to be. So I said to my wife, my pret-ty lit-tle wife, "Ex-plain this thing to me. What's this horse a do-in' in the sta-ble where my horse ought to be?" (She) You darn fool, you drun-ken fool, can't you nev-er see? It's noth-in' but a milk cow that your mo-ther gave to me." (He) Well, I've tra-veled this wide world o-ver, ten thou-sand miles or more, but a sad-dle on a milk cow I nev-er did see be- fore.

The second night, I got home, drunk as I could be,
I spied a hat on the hatrack, where my hat ought to be.
I says to my wife, my pretty little wife, "Explain this thing to me,
What's this hat doing here on the hatrack, where my hat ought to be?"
"You blind fool, you drunken old fool, can't you never see,
That's nothing but an old chamber pot my granny gave to me."
I traveled this wide world over, ten thousand miles or more,
And a J. B. Stetson chamber pot, I never did see before.

I got home the third night, drunk as I could be,
I spied some pants upon the chair where my pants ought to be.
I says to my wife, my pretty little wife, "Explain this thing to me,
What's these pants doing here upon the chair, where my pants ought to be?"
"You blind fool, you drunken old fool, can't you never see,
That's nothing but an old dish rag, my granny gave to me."
I've traveled this wide world over, ten thousand miles or more,
And zippers on a dishrag I never did see before.

I got home the fourth night, drunk as
    I could be,
I spied a head on the pillow, where my
    head ought to be.
I says to my wife, my pretty little
    wife, "Explain this thing to me,
What's this head doing here on the
    pillow, where my head ought
    to be?"

"You blind fool, you drunken old fool,
    can't you plainly see,
That's nothing but an old cabbage
    head, my granny gave to me."
I've traveled this wide world over,
    ten thousand miles or more,
And a mustache on a cabbage head I
    never did see before.

Well, the fifth night, I got home,
    drunk as I could . . . .

Cielito Lindo

It was probably composed in the 19th Century, when Italian
opera had a great influence on Mexican popular song.

1. De la Sie - rra Mo - re-na, Cie - li-to Lin - do vie-
nen ba - jan - do ___ Un par de o - ji - tos ne - gros, Cie-
li-to Lin-do, los___ con-tra- ban-do ___ Ay, Ay, Ay,
Ay ___ Can - ta y no llo - res, Por - que can-tan-do se a-
le-gran, Cie - li-to Lin-do los___ cor - a - zo - nes.

El amor es un bicho,
cielito lindo, que cuando pica
No se encuentra remedio,
cielito lindo, en la botica
Ay, ay, etc.

Love is a bug, Cielito Lindo,
When it bites there is no remedy,
Cielito Lindo,
In the drugstore

Come All You Fair
And Tender Ladies

(Cecil Sharp collected many versions of this song, and printed them in his book "English Folk Songs in the Southern Appalachians." This is a somewhat composite version.)

(See page 4 for acknowledgement of printed source.)

Freely

Come all ye fair and ten-der la-dies, take warn- ing how you court young men. They're like the stars of a summer's morn-ing; They'll first ap- pear and then they're gone.

If I'd ha' known before I courted,
I never would have courted none.
I'd have locked my heart in a box of
golden
And fastened it up with a silver pin.

I wish I were a little swallow,
And I had wings and I could fly.
I would fly away to my false-true lover
And when he would speak I would deny.

But I am not a little swallow,
I have no wings neither can I fly.
So I'll sit down here to weep in sorrow
And try to pass my troubles by.

Oh don't you remember our days
of courting,
When your head lay upon my breast?
You could make me believe by the fal-
ling of your arm,
That the sun rose in the west.

Come all ye fair and tender ladies,
Take warning how you court young men.
They are like the stars of a summer's
morning
They will first appear and then they
are gone.

I Ride An Old Paint

(Dances in Western Oklahoma used to end with this slow waltz. Margaret Larkin printed it in her early book of cowboy songs, and Carl Sandburg got it from her.)

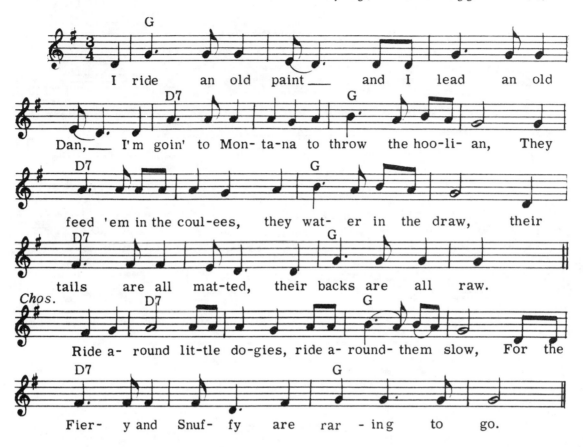

I ride an old paint ___ and I lead an old Dan, ___ I'm goin' to Mon-ta-na to throw the hoo-li-an, They feed 'em in the coul-ees, they wat-er in the draw, their tails are all mat-ted, their backs are all raw.

Chos. Ride a-round lit-tle do-gies, ride a-round them slow, For the Fier-y and Snuf-fy are rar-ing to go.

Old Bill Jones had a daughter and a
    son
Son went to college and the daughter
    went wrong
His wife got killed in a pool-room fight
Still he keeps singing from morning
    till night.   (Cho.)

When I die take my saddle from the
    wall
Put it on to my pony lead him out of
    his stall
Tie my bones to his back turn our
    faces to the west
And we'll ride the prairie that we love
    the best.   (Cho.)

Home On The Range

(Printed by John Lomax in his first book of cowboy songs, this became the subject of a big lawsuit in the 1920's, when millions of records of the song were first sold. Authorship of a sort was finally traced to the midwest, circa 1880.)

Oh give me a home, where the buf- fa- lo roam, Where the deer and the an- te- lope play,____ Where sel- dom is heard a dis- cour- ag- ing word, And the skies are not clou- dy all day.____

Chorus

Home, home on the range,____ Where the deer and the an- te- lope play, ____ where sel- dom is heard a dis- cour- ag- ing word, and the skies are not cloud- y all day.____

How often at night when the heavens
    are bright
With the light of the glittering stars,
I stood there amazed and I asked as I
    gazed
Does their glory exceed that of ours? (Cho.)

Clementine

(A popular song of the California gold rush of 1849. The tune is probably much older. Sounds German to me, but I've been told it was Mexican, early 19th Century.)

In a ca-vern, in a can-yon, ex-ca-va-ting for a mine, lived a min-er, for-ty nin-er, and his daugh-ter, Clem-en-tine.

Chos.

Oh, my dar-ling, Oh, my dar-ling, Oh, my dar-ling, Clem-en-tine, you are lost and gone for-ev-er, Dread-ful sor-ry, Clem-en-tine.

Light she was and, like a fairy, and
  her shoes were number nine,
Herring boxes, without topses, sandals
  were for Clementine.   (Cho.)

Drove she ducklings to the water,
  every morning just at nine,
Stubbed her toe upon a splinter, fell
  into the foaming brine.   (Cho.)

Ruby lips above the water, blowing
  bubbles soft and fine,
But alas I was no swimmer, so I lost
  my Clementine.   (Cho.)

There's a churchyard, on the hillside,
  where the flowers grow and twine,
There grow roses, 'mongst the posies,
  fertilized by Clementine.   (Cho.)

Little Girl

(One of the many fine songs I learned from Huddie Ledbetter ("Leadbelly"). Like so many folksongs, it appears to be a fragment, and its unclear meaning may be part of the magic. Leadbelly used to sing it "Black girl, black girl" and some prefer it that way.)

(See page 4 for acknowledgement of printed source.)

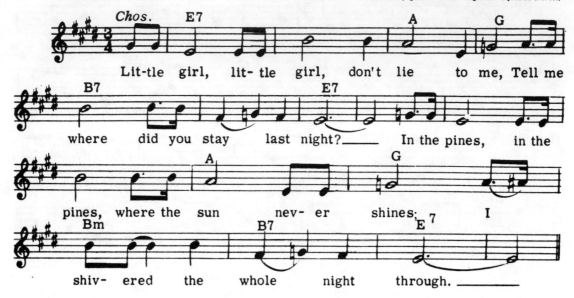

Lit-tle girl, lit-tle girl, don't lie to me, Tell me where did you stay last night?___ In the pines, in the pines, where the sun nev-er shines; I shiv-ered the whole night through. ___

You cause me to weep, you cause me
   to moan,
You cause me to leave my home.
I wish to the Lord, I'd never seen
   your face
I'm sorry you ever was born.

My husband was a railroad man,
Died a mile and a half from town.
His head was found in the driver's
   wheel,
And his body it never was found.

(Repeat first verse)

I Never Will Marry

(The Carter Family recorded this in the 1930's, and Mrs. Texas Gladden also. It probably has an 18th Century English origin. I wish it had more verses! You can string it out longer by singing the chorus halfway through the 2nd verse, as well as at the end.)

(See page 4 for acknowledgement of printed source.)

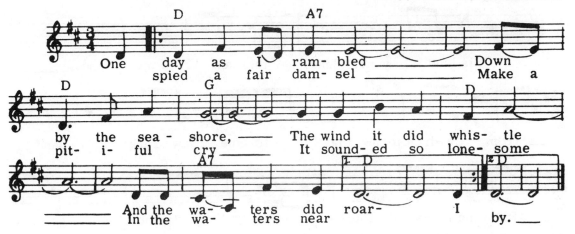

One day as I ram-bled _____ Down
spied a fair dam-sel _____ Make a

by the sea - shore, _____ The wind it did whis - tle
pit - i - ful cry _____ It sound - ed so lone - some

_____ And the wa - ters did roar-
_____ In the wa - ters near _____ by. _____

Chorus:
I never will marry, I'll be no man's wife,
I expect to live single, all the days of my life.
The shells in the ocean, will be my death bed,
The fish in deep water, swim over my head.

My love's gone and left me, he's the one I adore,
He's gone where I never shall see him any more.
She plunged her dear body, in the water so deep,
She closed her pretty blue eyes, in the waters to sleep. (Cho.)

This Land Is Your Land

(Another from America's greatest contemporary ballad maker, Woody Guthrie. He travelled the length and breadth of this land, often without a dime in his pocket, making up songs like this.)

(See page 4 for acknowledgement of printed source.)

As I went walking that ribbon of high-
    way
I saw above me that endless skyway,
I saw below me that golden valley,
This land was made for you and me.

Chorus

I roamed and rambled, and I
    followed my footsteps,
To the sparkling sands of her diamond
    deserts,
All around me a voice was sounding,
This land was made for you and me.

Chorus

When the sun come shining, then I was
    strolling,
And the wheat fields waving, and the
    dust clouds rolling,
A voice was chanting as the fog was
    lifting,
This land was made for you and me.

Chorus

In the squares of the city by the
    shadow of the steeple
Near the relief office I saw my
    people
And some were stumbling and some
    were wondering if
This land was made for you and me.

Chorus

As I went rambling that dusty
    highway
I saw a sign that said private
    property
But on the other side it didn't say
    nothing
This land was made for you and me.

Chorus

Nobody living can ever stop me
As I go walking my freedom
    highway
Nobody living can make me turn
    back
This land was made for you and me.

Passing Through

Words and adaptation by Dick Blakeslee. Copyright 1948 by Dick Blakeslee.

I saw Ad-am leave the gar-den, with an ap-ple in his
I saw Je-sus on the cross, on that hill called Calvary,

hand, I said, "Now you're out, what are you gon-na do?"
"Do you hate man-kind for what they done to you?"

"Plant my crops and pray for rain, may-be
He said, "Talk of love not hate, things to

raise a lit-tle Cain, I'm an or-phan now and
do it's gettin' late, I've so lit-tle time and

on-ly pass-ing through." Pass-ing through,
I'm just pass-ing

pass-ing through, some-times hap-py, some-times

blue, glad that I ran in-to you; tell the

peo-ple that you saw me pass-ing through.

Well, I shivered with George Washing-
ton, one night at Valley Forge,
Why do the soldiers freeze here like
they do?
He said, "Men will suffer, fight,
Even die for what is right,
Even though they know they're only
passing through." (Cho.)

I was at Franklin Roosevelt's side,
just a while before he died,
He said, "One world must come out of
World War II;
Yankee, Russian, white or tan,
Lord, a man is just a man,
We're all brothers and we're only
passing through." (Cho.)

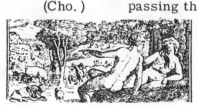

Strangest Dream

(Words and music by the Canadian singer, Ed McCurdy.)

(See page 4 for acknowledgement of printed source.)

Last night I had the strang-est dream, I'd nev- er dreamed be- fore;___ I dreamed the world had all a-greed to put an end to war.___ I dreamed I saw a might- y room, the room was full of men,___ and the pa- per they were sign-ing said, they'd nev-er fight a-gain.

And when the paper was all signed
And a million copies made,
They all joined hands and bowed their heads
And grateful prayers were prayed.

And the people in the streets below
Were dancing round and round,
And swords and guns and uniforms
We re scattered on the ground.

(Repeat first verse)

Down In The Valley

(Another Southern mountain version of an older song from England, Ireland, or Scotland.)

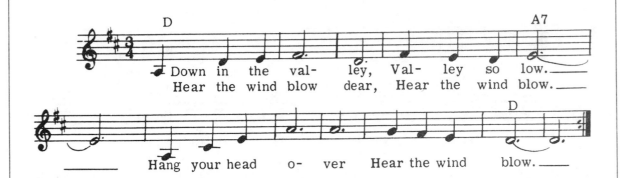

Down in the val - ley, Val - ley so low.
Hear the wind blow dear, Hear the wind blow.

_____ Hang your head o - ver Hear the wind blow. _____

Roses love sunshine, violets love dew
Angels in heaven, know I love you.
Know I love you dear, know I love you
Angels in heaven, know I love you.

If you don't love me, love whom you
    please
Throw your arms round me, give my
    heart ease.
Give my heart ease love, give my
    heart ease
Throw your arms round me, give my
    heart ease.

Build me a castle forty feet high
So I can see him as he rides by.
As he rides by love, as he rides by
So I can see him as he rides by.

Write me a letter, send it by mail
Send it in care of Birmingham jail.
Birmingham jail love, Birmingham
    jail
Send it in care of Birmingham jail.

(Repeat first verse)

CRADLING

NUT-GATHERING

CUTTING CORN

WHEAT HARVEST

Buffalo Gals

(Another folk descendant of a popular 19th Century minstrel song.)

As I was walk-ing down the street,
Down the street, Down the street, A pret-ty lit-tle girl I
chanced to meet, And we danced by the light of the moon.
Chos. Buf-fa-lo gal won't you come out to-night, Come out to-night.
Come out to - night? Buf-fa- lo gal won't you
come out to-night, And dance by the light of the moon?

I danced with a gal with a hole in her
 stocking
And her heel kept a-knockin' and her
 toes kept a-rocking
I danced with a gal with a hole in her
 stocking
And we danced by the light of the
 moon.   (Cho.)

34

Old Joe Clark

(A classic banjo tune. Note the flatted 7th note of the scale. Joe Clark was an actual person, a veteran of the War of 1812.)

Old Joe Clark's a fine old man, Tell you the rea- son

why, He keeps good lik-ker 'round his house, Good old Rock and

Rye. Fare ye well, Old Joe Clark, Fare ye well, I say.

Fare ye well, Old Joe Clark, I'm a- goin' a- way.

Old Joe Clark, the preacher's son,
Preached all over the plain,
The only text he ever knew
Was "High, low jack and the game."
(Cho.)

Old Joe Clark had a mule,
His name was Morgan Brown,
And every tooth in that mule's head
Was sixteen inches around.   (Cho.)

Old Joe Clark had a yellow cat,
She would neither sing or pray,
She stuck her head in the buttermilk
   jar
And washed her sins away.   (Cho.)

Old Joe Clark had a house
Fifteen stories high,
And every storey in that house
Was filled with chicken pie.   (Cho.)

I went down to old Joe's house,
He invited me to supper,
I stumped my toe on the table leg
And stuck my nose in the butter. (Cho.)

Now I wouldn't marry a widder,
Tell you the reason why,
She'd have so many children
They'd make those biscuits fly.   (Cho.)

Sixteen horses in my team,
The leaders they are blind,
And every time the sun goes down
There's a pretty girl on my mind.
(Cho.)

Eighteen miles of mountain road
And fifteen miles of sand,
If I ever travel this road again,
I'll be a married man.   (Cho.)

Jesse James

(Jesse James, The Missouri train robber, was living under an alias of Mr. Howard when he was shot by a former member of his band.)

Jes-se James was a lad, he killed man-y a man, He robbed the Glen-dale train; He took from the rich and he gave to the poor, He'd a hand and a heart and a brain. Oh

Chorus

Jes-se had a wife to mourn for his life, Three child-ren they were brave; But that dir-ty lit-tle cow-ard that shot Mis-ter How-ard, He laid poor Jes-se in his grave.

It was on a Saturday night and the
   moon was shining bright,
They robbed the Glendale train,
With the agent on his knees, he
   delivered up the keys
To these outlaws Frank and Jesse
   James. (Cho.)

The people held their breath when they
   heard of Jesse's death
They wondered how he ever came to
   fall;
Robert Ford, it was a fact, shot Jesse
   in the back
While Jesse hung a picture on the
   wall. (Cho.)

Oh, Jesse was a man, a friend of the
   poor
He'd never rob a mother or a child;
He took from the rich and he gave to
   the poor
So they shot Jesse James on the sly.
   (Cho.)

Well, this song was made by Billy
   Gashade,
As soon as the news did arrive;
He said there was no man with the law
   in his hand
Who could take Jesse James when
   alive. (Cho.)

Joshua Fought
The Battle Of Jericho

(Many Negro spirituals, I've found, take on new poetic meanings, as life reveals new facets in them. It is as though the song is born anew with each successive generation.)

Up to the walls of Jericho
He marched with spear in hand,
"Go blow those ram-horns," Joshua
    cried,
"Cause the battle is in my hands."
                        (Cho.)

Then the lamb ram sheephorns began
    to blow,
The trumpets began to sound.
Joshua commanded the children to
    shout,
And the walls come a tumbling down.
                        (Cho.)

There's no man like Joshua
No man like Saul
No man like Joshua
At the battle of Jericho.   (Cho.)

We Shall Not Be Moved

(A spiritual which was born again in the union movement of the 1930's. The Southern Tenant Farmers Union started using it, and now it is thought of as a union song in many states.)

G D D7 G C
We shall not, we shall not be moved, We shall not, we shall not be moved, just like a tree that's stand-ing by the

G D7 G
wa- ter, We shall not be moved.

The union is behind us, we shall not
   be moved
The union is behind us, we shall not
   be moved
Just like a tree that's standing by the
   water
We shall not be moved.

We shall not, we shall not be moved
   (etc.)

We will stand and fight together, we
   shall not (etc.)

We shall not, we shall not be moved
   (etc.)

We are black and white together, we
   shall not (etc.)

Blow The Man Down

(Like many sea chanties, this one originally had verses not composed for tender ears. Paradise Street was in Liverpool. Many a sailor woke up after a hard night on the town to find himself aboard another ship bound to sea.)

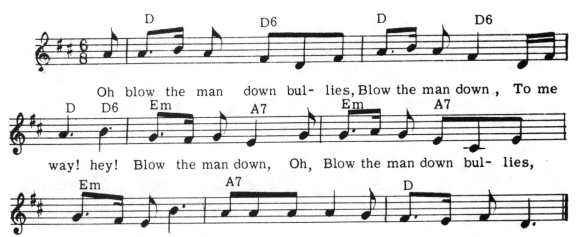

Oh blow the man down bul- lies, Blow the man down., To me way! hey! Blow the man down, Oh, Blow the man down bul- lies, Blow him a- way, Give me some time to blow the man down.

As I was a-walkin' down Paradise
Street,
To me way! hey! - Blow the man
down!
A pretty young damsel I chanced for
to meet,
Give me some time to blow the man
down. (Cho.)

She hailed me with her flipper, I took
her in tow,
To me way! hey! - Blow the man
down!
Yard-arm to yard-arm away we did go
Give me some time to blow the man
down. (Cho.)

As soon as that Packet was clear of
the bar,
To me way! hey! - Blow the man
down!
The mate knocked me down with the
end of a spar,
Give me some time to blow the man
down. (Cho.)

Its yard-arm to yard-arm away you
will sprawl,
Way! hey! - Blow the man down!
For kicking Jack Rogers commands
the Black Ball
Give me some time to blow the man
down. (Cho.)

The Camptown Races

(By Stephen Foster. His best songs grew out of folk tradition and got taken back into it.)

Chorus

Goin' to run all night, goin' to run all day, I bet my mon-ey on a bob-tailed nag, Some-bo-dy bet on the bay.

Verse

Oh, the Camp-town la-dies sing this song doo-da doo-da The Camp-town race track's two miles long, Oh, de doo-da day.

Oh, the long tailed filly and the big black horse,
Dooda, dooda,
Come to a mud hole and they all cut across,
Oh, de dooda day.   (Cho.)

I went down South with my hat caved in,
Dooda, dooda,
I come back North with a pocket full of tin,
Oh, de dooda day.   (Cho.)

The Streets of Laredo

(The Lomaxes, John and Alan, should take large credit for this song, I feel. It is just one of many hundreds of descendants of an 18th Century English broadside, "The Unfortunate Rake." But whereas most folksong collectors searched one small corner of the globe for the oldest songs they could find, Alan Lomax combed the whole U.S. for the best songs he could find. If necessary, he'd combine several half good songs to make one very good song. Bad folklore practice some claimed, but good editing, at least in this case.)

(See page 4 for acknowledgement of printed source.)

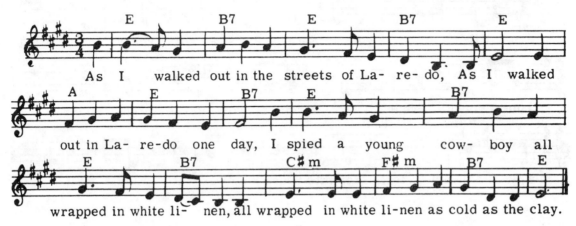

As I walked out in the streets of La- re- do, As I walked out in La- re- do one day, I spied a young cow- boy all wrapped in white li- nen, all wrapped in white li- nen as cold as the clay.

"I see by your outfit that you are a
  cowboy" —
These words he did say as I boldly
  stepped by,
"Come sit down beside me and hear
  my sad story;
I was shot in the breast and I know I
  must die.

"It was once in the saddle I used to go
  dashing,
It was once in the saddle I used to go
  gay;
First to the dram-house and then to
  the card-house;
Got shot in the breast; I am dying
  today.

"Get six jolly cowboys to carry my
  coffin;
Get six pretty maidens to carry my
  pall;
Put bunches of roses all over my
  coffin,
Roses to deaden the clods as they fall.

"Oh, beat the drum slowly and play the
  fife lowly,
Play the dead march as you carry me
  along;
Take me to the green valley and lay
  the sod o'er me,
For I'm a young cowboy and I know
  I've done wrong.

"Go fetch me a cup, a cup of cold
  water,
To cool my parched lips," the cowboy
  then said;
Before I returned, the spirit had left
  him
And gone to its Maker—the cowboy
  was dead.

We beat the drum slowly and played
  the fife lowly,
And bitterly wept as we bore him
  along;
For we all loved our comrade, so
  brave, young, and handsome,
We all loved our comrade although
  he'd done wrong.

Young Man Who Wouldn't Hoe Corn

(Another folksong first printed, of all things, by the Resettlement Administration, the New Deal agency of the 1930's.)

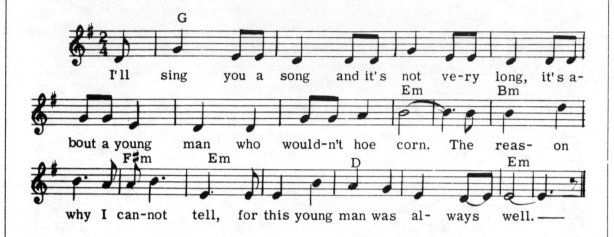

I'll sing you a song and it's not ve-ry long, it's a-bout a young man who would-n't hoe corn. The reas-on why I can-not tell, for this young man was al-ways well. ——

He planted his corn in the month of
   June,
And by July it was knee high;
First of September come a big frost,
And all this young man's corn was lost.

He went to the fence and there peeked
   in,
The weeds and the grass come up to
   his chin;
The weeds and the grass they grew so
   high,
It caused this young man for to sigh.

He went down to his neighbor's door,
Where he had often been before;
Saying, "Pretty little miss, will you
   marry me,
Pretty little miss what do you say."

Here you are a-wanting for to wed,
And cannot make your own cornbread;
Single I am, single I'll remain,
A lazy man I'll not maintain.

Well, he went down to the pretty little
   widder,
And I hope by heck that he don't git her;
She gave him the mitten sure as you're
   born
All because he wouldn't hoe corn.

Fillimeeooreay

(A popular song of 19th Century Irish immigrants. I learned it from Alan Lomax. I don't know where he learned it.)

(See page 4 for acknowledgement of printed source.)

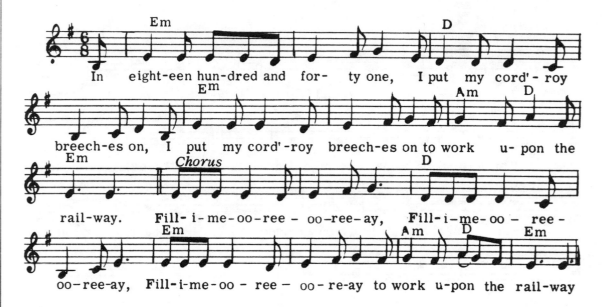

In eight-een hun-dred and for- ty one, I put my cord'- roy breech-es on, I put my cord'-roy breech-es on to work u- pon the rail-way.

Chorus

Fill- i-me-oo-ree - oo-ree-ay, Fill-i-me-oo - ree - oo-ree-ay, Fill-i-me-oo - ree — oo-re-ay to work u-pon the rail-way

In eighteen hundred and forty-two,
I left the old world for the new,
Bad cess to the luck that brought me
    through
To work upon the railway.

In eighteen hundred and forty-three
'Twas then I met sweet Biddy McGee
An elegant wife she's been to me
While working on the railway.

In eighteen hundred and forty-five,
I thought myself more dead than alive,
I thought myself more dead than alive
While working on the railway.

It's "Pat do this" and "Pat do that,"
Without a stocking or cravat,
Nothing but an old straw hat
While Pat worked on the railway.

In eighteen hundred and forty-seven,
Sweet Biddy McGee   she went to
    heaven,
If she left one kid, she left eleven,
To work upon the railway.

Alabama Bound

(From the singing of Huddie Ledbetter. He remade every song to fit his big 12-string guitar, with its booming bass notes.)

(See page 4 for acknowledgement of printed source.)

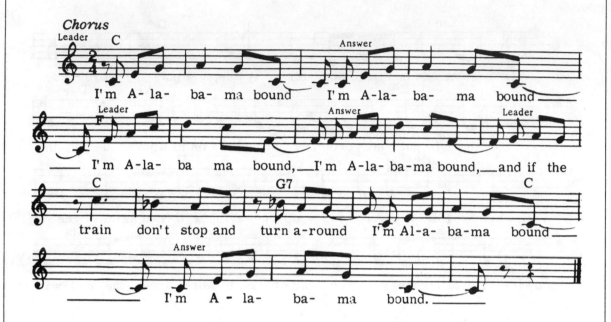

Chorus

I'm A-la-ba-ma bound I'm A-la-ba-ma bound ___ I'm A-la-ba ma bound, ___ I'm A-la-ba-ma bound, ___ and if the train don't stop and turn a-round I'm Al-a-ba-ma bound ___ I'm A-la-ba-ma bound. ___

Oh, don't you leave me here (repeat)
Oh, don't you leave me here (repeat)
But if you must go anyhow
Leave me a dime for beer. (repeat)

Chorus

Oh, don't you be like me (repeat)
Oh, don't you be like me (repeat)
You can drink your good Sherry wine
And let the whiskey be. (repeat)

Chorus

Aunt Rhody

(The tune has been traced to an opera (1752) by Jean Jacque Rousseau, and perhaps it pre-dates that.)

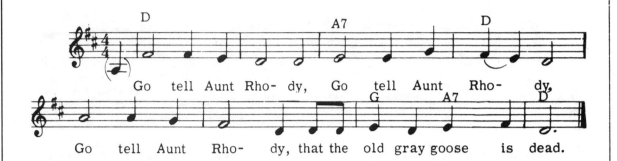

Go tell Aunt Rho-dy, Go tell Aunt Rho-dy,

Go tell Aunt Rho-dy, that the old gray goose is dead.

The one she's been saving (3)
To make a feather bed.

Old gander's weeping (3)
Because his wife is dead.

And the goslings are mourning (3)
Because their mother's dead.

She died in the mill-pond (3)
Standing on her head.

(Repeat first verse)

Oh, Susanna

(Probably Stephen Foster's greatest song, a ditty children will always love.)

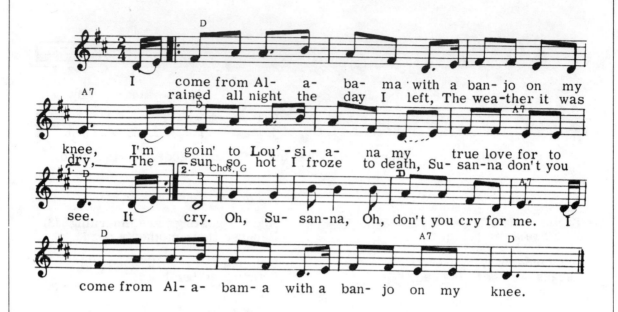

I come from Al-a-ba-ma with a banjo on my knee,
rained all night the day I left, The wea-ther it was

I'm goin' to Lou'-si-a-na my true love for to
dry,___ The sun so hot I froze to death, Su-san-na don't you

see. It cry. Oh, Su-san-na, Oh, don't you cry for me. I

come from Al-a-bam-a with a banjo on my knee.

I had a dream the other night, when everything was still
I dreamed I saw Susanna a-coming down the hill.

A red red rose was in her cheek, a tear was in her eye
I said to her, Susanna girl, Susanna don't you cry.   (Cho.)

Joe Bowers

(Another song of the 49'ers.)

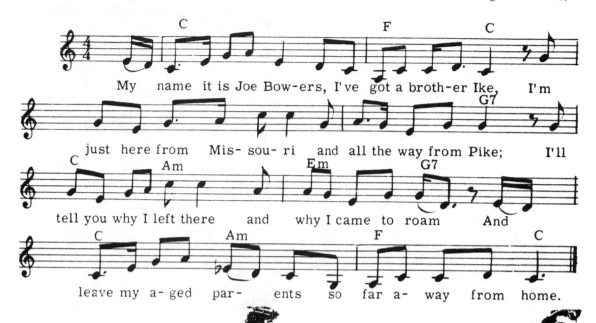

My name it is Joe Bow-ers, I've got a broth-er Ike, I'm just here from Mis-sou-ri and all the way from Pike; I'll tell you why I left there and why I came to roam And leave my a-ged par-ents so far a-way from home.

I used to court a girl there,
    her name was Sally Black,
I asked her if she'd marry,
    she said it was a whack;
She says to me, "Joe Bowers,
    before we've hitched for life,
You ought to get a little home
    to keep your little wife."

Says I, "My dearest Sally,
    Oh, Sally, for your sake,
I'll go to California and try to raise
    a stake."
Says she to me, "Joe Bowers,
    you're just the one to win."
She gave me a kiss to seal the bargain
    and throwed a dozen in.

I'll never forget my feelings when
    I bid adieu to all.
Sal she cotched me around the neck,
    and I began to bawl.
When I began they all commenced,
    you never heard the like,
How they took on and cried
    the day I left old Pike.

When I got to this country,
    I had nary a red;
I had such wolfish feelings,
    I wished myself most dead.
But the thoughts of my dear Sally
    soon made this feelin git.
And whispered hopes to Bowers,
    Lord, I wish I had 'em yet.

At last I went to mining,
    put in my biggest licks,
Came down upon the boulders
    just like a thousand bricks;
I worked both late and early,
    in rain, in sun and snow,
I was working for my Sally,
    'twas all the same to Joe.

One day I got a letter from
    my dear brother Ike,
It came from old Missouri
    all the way from Pike.
It brought me the darndest news
    that ever you did hear,
My heart it is a-breaking,
    so please excuse this tear.

It said my Sal was false to me,
    that her love for me had fled,
That she had got married to a butcher
    whose hair was red;
It told me more than that;
    it's enough to make me swear,
That Sal had had a baby
    and the baby had red hair.

Now I told you everything
    about this sad sad affair,
About Sally marrying the butcher
    and the baby had red hair;
But whether it was a boy or girl
    the letter never said,
It only said the baby's hair
    was inclined to be red.

Irene, Goodnight

(In 1950, six months after Leadbelly died, this song of his sold two million copies on the hit parade. He always said Irene was a real person and he knew her — a girl just sixteen years old, who met a rambler and a gambler.)

(See page 4 for acknowledgement of printed source.)

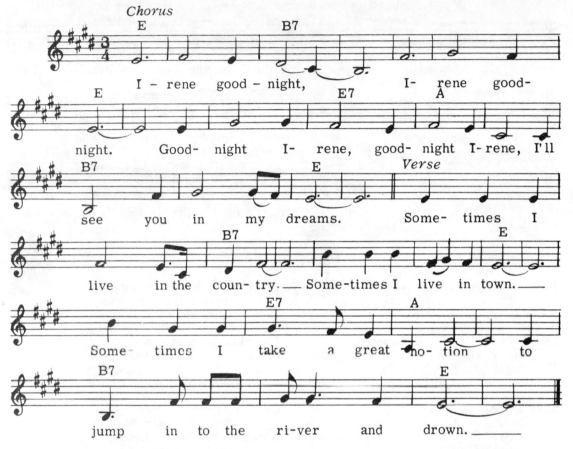

Chorus

I-rene good-night, I-rene good-night. Good-night I-rene, good-night I-rene, I'll see you in my dreams.

Verse

Some-times I live in the coun-try. Some-times I live in town. Some-times I take a great no-tion to jump in-to the ri-ver and drown.

I love Irene, God knows I do,
I'll love her till the seas run dry.
And if Irene turns her back on me,
I'd take morphine and die.   (Cho.)

I asked your mother for you,
She told me you was too young.
I wished to God I'd never seen your
    face,
I'm sorry you ever was born.   (Cho.)

You caused me to weep, you caused
    me to mourn,
You caused me to leave my home.
But the very last words I heard her say,
Was please sing me one more song.
                        (Cho.)

48

Sometimes I Feel Like A Motherless Child

(Perhaps the inhumanity of slavery can be first grasped by sensing the events behind a Negro Spiritual such as this. It was common practice to sell the children of slaves away from their parents.)

Slowly

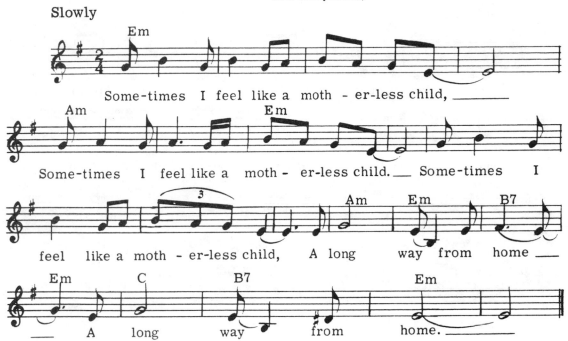

Some-times I feel like a moth-er-less child, _____

Some-times I feel like a moth-er-less child. _ Some-times I

feel like a moth-er-less child, A long way from home _

_ A long way from home. _____

Sometimes I feel like I'm almost gone. (3)
A long ways from home, a long ways from home.

Sometimes I feel like a feather in the air. (3)
A long ways from home, a long ways from home.

(Repeat first verse)

Study War No More

(Another old spiritual which has had a rebirth of meaning within the last few years.)

I'm gon-na lay down my sword and shield, down by the ri-ver side, down by the ri-ver side, down by the ri-ver-side, I'm gon- na lay down my sword and shield down by the ri-ver side, Gon- na stu-dy ____ war no more.__ I ain't gon-na stu-dy war no more, I ain't gon'-na stu-dy war no more, I ain't gonna stu-dy _____ war no more._____ I ain't gon-na more._____

I'm gonna walk with the Prince of Peace,
    down by the riverside,
    down by the riverside,
    down by the riverside,
I'm gonna walk with the Prince of Peace,
    down by the riverside,
And study war no more.   (Cho.)

Yes, I'm a'gonna shake hands around
    the world,
    down by the riverside,
    down by the riverside,
    down by the riverside,
I'm gonna shake hands around the
    world,
    down by the riverside,
And study war no more.   (Cho.)

Stagolee

(Learned from Woody Guthrie, in 1940. I think he got it from a phonograph record. Stagolee, of course, was supposed to have been an actual person around the turn of the century. Like "Frankie and Johnny" this song is also an example of a narrative ballad based on a honky tonk blues style.)

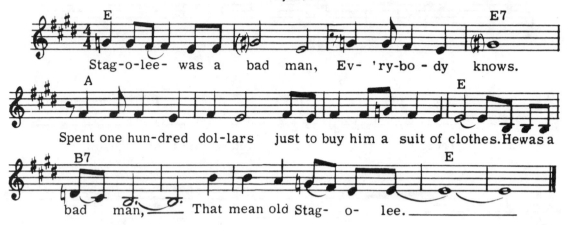

Stag-o-lee- was a bad man, Ev- 'ry-bo-dy knows.

Spent one hun-dred dol-lars just to buy him a suit of clothes. He was a

bad man,—— That mean old Stag- o- lee. ——————

Stagolee shot Billy de Lyons
What do you think about that,
Shot him down in cold blood
Because he stole his Stetson hat;
   He was a bad man
   That mean old Stagolee.

Billy de Lyons said, Stagolee
Please don't take my life,
I've got two little babes
And a darling, loving wife;
   You are a bad man
   You mean old Stagolee.

What do I care about your two little
   babes,
Your darling loving wife,
You done stole my Stetson hat
I'm bound to take your life;
   He was a bad man
   That mean old Stagolee.

The judge said, Stagolee
What you doing in here,
You done shot Mr. Billy de Lyons
You going to die in the electric chair;
   He was a bad man
   That mean old Stagolee.

Twelve o'clock they killed him
Head reached up high,
Last thing that poor boy said
My six-shooter never lied.
   He was a bad man
   That mean old Stagolee.

Old Dan Tucker

(By Dan Emmett, who also composed "Dixie." It was the big hit song of 1844 ("Oh Susanna" came in 1848) and is another example of a minstrel tune that got taken back into folk tradition, and further changed.)

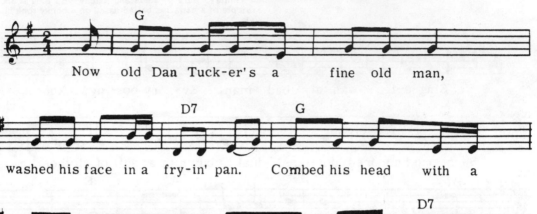

Now old Dan Tuck-er's a fine old man,

washed his face in a fry-in' pan. Combed his head with a

wag- on wheel, And died with a tooth ache in his heel.

Chos.
Get out the way old Dan Tuck- er, You're too late to

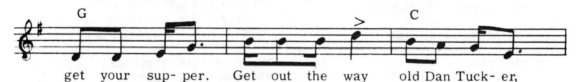

get your sup- per. Get out the way old Dan Tuck- er,

You're too late to get your sup- per.

Now old Dan Tucker is come to town
Riding a billy goat — leading a hound
Hound dog bark and the billy goat jump
Landed Dan Tucker on top of the stump.
(Cho.)

Now old Dan Tucker he got drunk
Fell in the fire and kicked up a chunk
Red hot coal got in his shoe
And oh my lawd how the ashes flew
(Cho.)

Now old Dan Tucker is come to town
Swinging the ladies round and round
First to the right and then to the left
Then to the girl that he loves best.
(Cho.)

Sally Ann

(Another good hoe-down. You better hunt up some more good verses for it.)

Did you e-ver see a mus-krat Sal-ly Ann? Pick-in' a ban- jo

Sal-ly Ann, drag-gin' his slick tail thru the sand? I'm gon-na mar-ry you

Chorus

Sal- ly Ann. I'm gon- na mar- ry you Sal, Sal,

I'm gon- na mar- ry you Sal- ly Ann.

Make my living in sandy land (3)
I'm gonna marry you, Sally Ann. (cho.)

Pick A Bale Of Cotton

(A good work song makes the long day seem shorter. In the fields this was sung medium slowly. Leadbelly made a party song out of it by speeding it up and adding a guitar accompaniment. It is a fun song.)

(See page 4 for acknowledgement of printed source.)

Oh, Lord-y, pick a bale of cot-ton. Oh, ___ Lord- y, pick a bale a day. pick a bale a day. Gon-na jump down turn a- round, pick a bale of cot-ton, Gon-na jump down turn a- round pick a bale a day, Gon- na pick a bale a day.

Gonna get on my knees . . .
   pick a bale of cotton,
Gonna get on my knees . . .
   pick a bale a day.
Gonna get on my knees . . .
   pick a bale of cotton,
Gonna get on my knees . . .
   pick a bale a day.   (Cho.)

Me and my gal gonna . . .
   pick a bale of cotton,
Me and my gal gonna . . .
   pick a bale a day.
Me and my gal gonna . . .
   pick a bale of cotton,
Me and my gal gonna . . .
   pick a bale a day.   (Cho.)

Gonna jump, jump, jump down . . .
   pick a bale of cotton,
Gonna jump down, turn around . . .
   pick a bale a day.
Gonna jump down, turn around . . .
   pick a bale of cotton,
Gonna jump down, turn around . . .
   pick a bale a day.   (Cho.)

Me and my buddy gonna . . .
   pick a bale of cotton,
Me and my buddy gonna . . .
   pick a bale a day.
Me and my buddy gonna . . .
   pick a bale of cotton,
Me and my buddy gonna . . .
   pick a bale a day.   (Cho.)

Gonna pick-a, pick-a, pick-a, pick-a . . .
   pick a bale of cotton,
Gonna pick-a, pick-a, pick-a, pick-a . . .
   pick a bale a day.
Gonna pick-a, pick-a, pick-a, pick-a . . .
   pick a bale of cotton,
We're gonna jump down, turn around . . .
   pick a bale a day.   (Cho.)

Midnight Special

(A widely known Southern prison song. Leadbelly taught us this version. I fixed up the last verse as a tribute to him. The song is supposed to be about a train that ran past the prison, and as the inmates listened to its hoarse freedom whistle they remembered a story that if the headlight should shine through the bars on a man, he'd go free.)

(See page 4 for acknowledgement of printed source.)

With sentiment, in a steady beat

1. Well, you wake up in the morn- ing,
2. If you go to Hous- ton,

Hear the ding-dong ring, You go a-march-ing to the
you bet-ter walk right; You bet-ter not

ta- ble, See the same damn thing; Well, it's on a one
stag- ger, You bet-ter not fight; Sher- iff Benson will ar-

ta- ble, Knife, a fork and a pan, And if you say any-thing a-
rest you, He'll car- ry you down, And if the jur- y finds you

bout it, You're in troub- le with the man.
Cho. guil- ty, Pen- i- ten- tia- ry bound.

Let the mid-night spe-cial Shine her light on me;

Let the mid-night spe-cial Shine her ev-er lov-ing light on me.

Yonder come little Rosie, how in the
world do you know,
I can tell her by her apron, and the
dress she wore.
Umbrella on her shoulder, piece of
paper in her hand,
She goes a-marching to the captain,
says I want my man. (Cho.)

Now old Huddie Ledbetter, he was a
mighty fine man,
Huddie taught this song to the whole
wide land.
But now he's done with all his grieving,
whooping, hollering and a-crying,
He's done with all his studying, about
his great long time. (Cho.)

Froggie Went A - Courtin'

(When singing this to children you can ask them to repeat "A-huh" after you each time.)

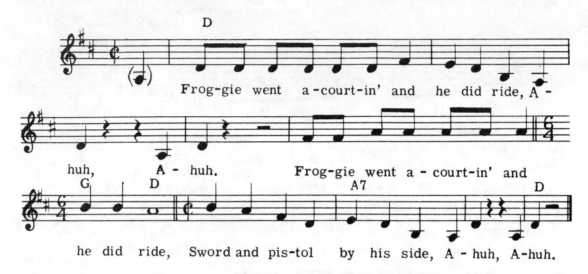

Frog-gie went a-court-in' and he did ride, A-huh, A-huh. Frog-gie went a-court-in' and he did ride, Sword and pis-tol by his side, A-huh, A-huh.

Well, he rode down to Miss Mouse's
  door, a-huh, a-huh,
Well, he rode down to Miss Mouse's
  door,
Where he had often been before, a-huh,
  a-huh.

He took Miss Mousie on his knee,
  a-huh, a-huh,
He took Miss Mousie on his knee,
Said, "Miss Mousie will you marry
  me?" A-huh, a-huh.

Similarly:

"I'll have to ask my Uncle Rat,
See what he will say to that."

"Without my Uncle Rat's consent,
I would not marry the President."

Well, Uncle Rat laughed and shook his
  fat sides,
To think his niece would be a bride.

Well, Uncle Rat rode off to town
To buy his niece a wedding gown.

"Where will the wedding supper be?"
"Way down yonder in a hollow tree."

"What will the wedding supper be?"
"A fried mosquito and a roasted flea."

First to come in were two little ants,
Fixing around to have a dance.

Next to come in was a bumble bee,
Bouncing a fiddle on his knee.

Next to come in was a fat sassy lad,
Thinks himself as big as his dad.

Thinks himself a man indeed,
Because he chews the tobacco weed.

And next to come in was a big tomcat,
He swallowed the frog and the mouse
  and the rat.

Next to come in was a big old snake,
He chased the party into the lake.

The Farmer Is The Man

(A popular song with the midwestern farmers of the 1880's, the days of the Farmer's Alliance, the Greenback Party, and the founding of the Grange movement.)

1. When the farm-er comes to town With his
2. When the law-yer hangs a-round While the

wag-on bro-ken down, Oh, the farm-er is the man who feeds them
butch-er cuts a pound, Oh, the farm-er is the man who feeds them

all. If you'll on-ly look and see, I
all. And the preach-er and the cook Go a-

think you will a-gree That the farm-er is the man who feeds them
stroll-ing by the brook, Oh, the farm-er is the man who feeds them

Refrain

all. The farm-er is the man, The farm-er is the man,

lives on cred-it till the fall;— {Then they take him by the hand, And they
{With the int-'rest rate so high, It's a

lead him from the land, And the mid-dle man's the one who gets it all.
won-der he don't die, For the mort-gage man's the one who gets it all.

When the banker says he's broke
And the merchant's up in smoke,
They forget that it's the farmer
  feeds them all.
It would put them to the test
If the farmer took a rest,
Then they'd know that it's the farmer
  feeds them all.

Oh, The farmer is the man,
The farmer is the man,
Lives on credit till the fall.
And his pants are wearing thin,
His condition it's a sin,
He's forgot that he's the man who
  feeds them all.

The Devil And The Farmer's Wife

(One more U.S. version of an old Scottish comic ballad. I learned it this way from Lee Hays, who learned it from someone in Arkansas.)

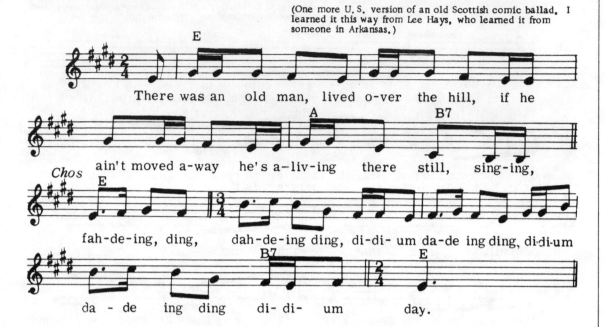

There was an old man, lived o-ver the hill, if he ain't moved a-way he's a-liv-ing there still, sing-ing,

Chos

fah-de-ing, ding, dah-de-ing ding, di-di- um da-de ing ding, di-di-um da - de ing ding di- di- um day.

Well, the devil came up to him one
    day,
Said one of your family I'm gonna take
    away.
Singing . . . . . . etc.

Oh please don't take my eldest son,
There's work on the farm that's gotta
    be done.
Singing . . . . . . etc.

It's all I want, that wife of yours,
Well you can take her with all of my
    heart.
Singing . . . . . . etc.

Well, he picks the wife up upon his
    back,
And off to hell he goes clickitty-clack.
Singing . . . . . . etc.

He carries her on about a mile down
    the road,
He said old woman you're a devil of a
    load.
Singing . . . . . . etc.

He carries her down to the gates of
    hell,
He says poke up the fire we'll scorch
    her well.
Singing . . . . . . etc.

Ther were two little devils with ball
    and with chain,
She ups with her foot and she kicks out
    their brains.
Singing . . . . . . etc.

And nine little devils went climbing up
    the wall,
Saying take her back daddy, she'll
    murder us all.
Singing . . . . . . etc.

Well, I got up next morning, I spied
    through a crack
I seen the old devil come a dragging
    her back.
Singing . . . . . . etc.

He said here is your wife, both sound
    and well,
If I'd a kept her there longer she'd a
    torn up hell.
Singing . . . . . . etc.

He said I've been a devil most all of
    my life,
But I'd never been in hell till I met
    with your wife.
Singing . . . . . . etc.

Now, this only goes to show, what a
    woman can do,
She can whup out the devil and her
    husband too.
Singing . . . . . . etc.

This shows that the women are better
    than men,
They can go down to hell and come
    back again.
Singing . . . . . . etc.

The Keeper

(A song from our British cousins, lots of fun as an answer-back song.)

mf

1 The keep- er did a hunt- ing go, And
2 The first doe she did cross the plain, The
3 The sec- ond doe she cross'd the brook: The

un- der his coat he car- ried a bow,
keep- er___ fetched her back ___ a- gain;
keep- er___ fetched her back ___ with his hook

All for to shoot at a mer- rie lit- tle doe. A-
Where she is now she___ may___ re- main, A-
Where she is now you may go ___ and look, A-

Chorus

1st. Voice   2nd.

mong the leaves so green, O. Jack- ie boy! (Mas- ter)

1   2   1   2

f
Sing ye well? (Ver- y well.)   Hey down (Ho down!)

1   A7 All D   A7 D 1

Der- ry, der- ry down, A- mong the leaves so green, O, *mf* To my

D   2

hey down, down! (To my   ho down, down!) *f* Hey down (Ho down!)

1   A7 All D   A7 D

Der- ry, der- ry down. A- mong the leaves so-green, O

59

On Top Of Old Smoky

In Adam's fall
We sinned all.

(The first version given here shows how some songs can be adapted slightly for group singing. At the bottom is the tune as it sounds better sung in the old solo way. I learned it from someone in the Smoky Mountains. Certain verses go back to Elizabethan times.)

On top of old Smo - ky, (all covered with snow) All cov-ered with

snow. (I lost my true lover) I lost my true lov-er (from courting too slow)

from court-ing so slow. (Now courting is pleasure) Now court-ing is pleas-

ure, (And parting is grief) And part-ing is grief (And a false hearted lover) And a

false hearted lov-er (is worse than a thief) is worse than a thief._____

Say a thief will just rob you and take
what you have
But a false hearted lover will lead you
to the grave.
And the grave will decay you and turn
you to dust
Not one boy in a hundred a poor girl
can trust.

They'll hug you and kiss you and tell
you more lies
Than the cross-ties on the railroad or
the stars in the skies.

So come all you young maidens and
listen to me
Never place your affection on a green
willow tree.

For the leaves they will wither and the
roots they will die
You'll all be forsaken and never know
why.
On top of Old Smoky all covered with
snow
I lost my true lover from courting to
slow.

2nd Version

On top of old Smok- y,   all cov-ered with snow, _____   I

lost my true lov-er, _____ from court-ing too slow.   Now court-ing is

pleas-ure,   and part-ing is grief, _____ and a false   heart- ed

lov-er,   is worse than a thief.

Cindy

(I first heard Bascom Lunsford sing this at Asheville, North Carolina, in 1935. Like other good banjo tunes, its verses can go on almost indefinitely.)

Quite fast

You ought to see my Cin-dy, She lives way down south;

She's so sweet the hon-ey bees Swarm a-round her mouth. Get-a- long

home, Cin-dy, Cin-dy, Get a-long home, Cin-dy, Cin-dy, Get a-long

home, Cin-dy, Cin-dy, I'll mar-ry you some day.

The first I seen my Cindy
She was standing in the door,
Her shoes and stockings in her hand,
Her feet all over the floor. (Cho.)

She took me to her parlor,
She cooled me with her fan;
She said I was the prettiest thing
In the shape of mortal man. (Cho.)

She kissed me and she hugged me,
She called me sugar plum;
She throwed her arms around me,
I thought my time had come. (Cho.)

Oh, Cindy is a pretty girl,
Cindy is a peach.
She threw her arms around my neck,
And hung on like a leech. (Cho.)

And if I was a sugar tree
Standing in the town,
Every time my Cindy passed
I'd shake some sugar down. (Cho.)

And if I had a thread and needle
Fine as I could sew,
I'd sew that gal to my coat tails
And down the road I'd go. (Cho.)

I wish I was an apple
A-hanging on a tree,
Every time that Cindy passed,
She'd take a bite of me. (Cho.)

John Brown's Body

(How many who sing this now realize that it was once an extremely controversial song about a most controversial man? I have purposely included one verse of Julia Ward Howe's "Battle Hymn of the Republic.")

John Brown's bo-dy lies a mould-'rin' in the grave,

John Brown's bo-dy lies a mould-'rin' in the grave,

John Brown's bo-dy lies a mould'rin' in the grave, But his

soul goes march-ing on. Glo-ry glo-ry hal-le lu-jah,

Glo-ry glo-ry hal-le lu-jah, Glo-ry glo-ry hal-le

lu-jah, But his soul goes march-ing on.

The stars above in heaven are a'lookin'
   kindly down, (3)
On the grave of old John Brown. (Cho.)

He captured Harper's Ferry with his
   nineteen men so true,
He frightened Old Virginia till she
   trembled through and through,
They hanged him for a traitor, they
   tnemselves the traitor crew,
But his soul goes marching on. (Cho.)

Well, he's gone to be a soldier in the
   army of the Lord, (3)
But his soul goes marching on. (Cho.)

Mine eyes have seen the glory of the
   coming of the Lord,
He's trampling out the vintage where
   the grapes of wrath are stored,
He's loosed the fateful lightning of his
   terrible, swift sword,
His truth is marching on. (Cho.)

Buffalo Skinners

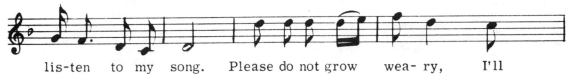

Steady Tempo   Dm

Come all you old-time cow-boys and lis-ten to my song. Please do not grow wea-ry, I'll not de-tain you long; Con-cern-ing some wild cow-boys who did a-gree to go and spend the sum-mer plea-sant on the trail of the buf-fa-lo.

I found myself in Griffin in the Spring
 of '83,
When a well-known, famous drover
 come a-walking up to me,
Saying, "How do you do, young feller,
 and how would you like to go,
"And spend a summer pleasant on the
 trail of the buffalo?"

Well, me being out of work right then,
 to the drover I did say,
"This going out on the buffalo range
 depends upon your pay.
"But if you will pay good wages —
 transportation to and fro,
"I think I might go with you to the trail
 of the buffalo."

"Of course I'll pay good wages —
 give transportation too,
"If you'll agree to work for me until
 the season's through.
"But if you do grow weary, and you
 try to run away,
"You'll starve to death along the trail,
 and also lose your way."

Well with all his flattering talking,
 he signed up quite a train,
Some ten or twelve in number —
 some able-bodied men.
Our trip it was a pleasant one as we
 hit the westward road,
And crossed old Boggy Creek in old
 New Mexico.

There our pleasures ended and our
 troubles all begun.
A lightning storm did hit us, and made
 our cattle run.
Got all full of stickers from the cactus
 that did grow,
And outlaws waiting to pick us off in
 the hills of Mexico.

Well, the working season ended and
 the drover would not pay.
"You all have drunk too much, you're
 all in debt to me."
But the cowboys never had heard of
 such a thing as a bankrupt law,
So we left that drover's bones to bleach
 on the trail of the buffalo.

Frankie And Johnny

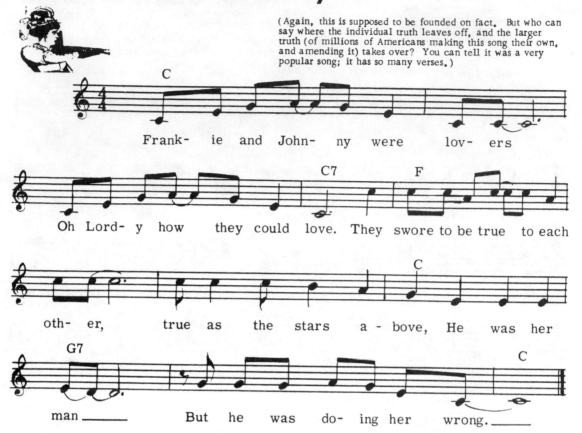

(Again, this is supposed to be founded on fact. But who can say where the individual truth leaves off, and the larger truth (of millions of Americans making this song their own, and amending it) takes over? You can tell it was a very popular song; it has so many verses.)

C

Frank- ie and John- ny were lov- ers

C7   **F**

Oh Lord- y how they could love. They swore to be true to each

C

oth- er, true as the stars a - bove, He was her

G7   **C**

man _____ But he was do- ing her wrong. _____

Frankie she was a good woman
As everybody knows,
Spent a hundred dollars
Just to buy her man some clothes.
He was her man, but he was doing her
   wrong.

Frankie went down to the corner
Just for a bucket of beer,
Said: "Mr. bartender
Has my loving Johnny been here?
"He was my man, but he's a-doing me
   wrong."

"Now I don't want to tell you no stories
And I don't want to tell you no lies
I saw your man about an hour ago
With a gal named Nellie Bligh
He was your man, but he's a-doing you
   wrong."

Frankie she went down to the hotel
Didn't go there for fun,
Underneath her kimona
She carried a forty-four gun.
He was her man, but he was doing her
   wrong.

Frankie looked over the transom
To see what she could spy,
There sat Johnny on the sofa
Just loving up Nellie Bligh.
He was her man, but he was doing her
   wrong.

Frankie got down from that high stool
She didn't want to see no more;
Rooty-toot-toot three times she shot
Right through that hardwood door.
He was her man, but he was doing her
   wrong.

Now the first time that Frankie shot
   Johnny
He let out an awful yell,
Second time she shot him
There was a new man's face in hell.
He was her man, but he was doing her
   wrong.

"Oh roll me over easy
Roll me over slow
Roll me over on the right side
For the left side hurts me so."
He was her man, but he was doing her
   wrong.

64

Sixteen rubber-tired carriages
Sixteen rubber-tired hacks
They take poor Johnny to the graveyard
They ain't gonna bring him back.
He was her man, but he was doing her
  wrong.

Frankie looked out of the jailhouse
To see what she could see,
All she could hear was a two-string
  bow
Crying nearer my God to thee.
He was her man, but he was doing her
  wrong.

Frankie she said to the sheriff,
"What do you reckon they'll do?"
Sheriff he said "Frankie,
It's the electric chair for you."
He was her man, but he was doing her
  wrong.

This story has no moral
This story has no end
This story only goes to show
That there ain't no good in men!
He was her man, but he was doing her
  wrong.

Who's Gonna Shoe Your Pretty Little Foot?

(A love-song, a lullaby, a fragment from the fifteenth century, remade and passed on to me by Woody Guthrie of Oklahoma and Brooklyn.)

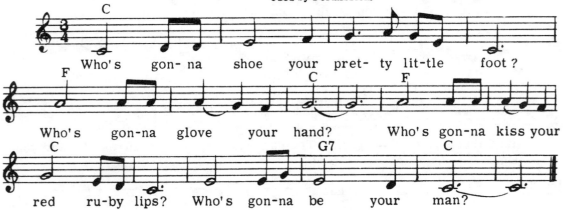

Who's gon-na shoe your pret-ty lit-tle foot?
Who's gon-na glove your hand? Who's gon-na kiss your
red ru-by lips? Who's gon-na be your man?

Papa will shoe my pretty little foot,
Mama will glove my hand,
Sister's gonna kiss my red ruby lips,
I don't need no man.

I don't need no man, poor boy,
I don't need no man.
Sister's gonna kiss my red ruby
  lips
I don't need no man.

Longest train I ever did see,
Was sixteen coaches long.
The only girl I ever did love,
Was on that train and gone.

The Big Rock Candy Mountain

(A hobo jungle was usually a patch of ground near the railroad tracks, a few hundred yards from town, where tramps,
hobos, and migrants would camp overnight, waiting for the
right freight train to take them out. A "shack" is a brake-
man on a freight train. A railroad bull is a company
policeman whose job is to chase away hoboes.)

Introduction

One eve-ning as the sun went down and the jun-gle fires were
burn-ing Down the track came a ho-bo hik-ing.— He said "Boys I'm not
turn-ing; I'm head-ing for a land that's far a-way be-side that cry-stal
foun-tain. I'll see you all this com-ing fall in the Big Rock Can-dy
Moun-tains. In the Big Rock Can-dy Moun-tains, it's a
land that's fair and bright, The hand-outs grow on bush-es and you
sleep out ev'-ry night; The box-cars all are emp-ty and the sun shines
day. I'm bound to go where there ain't no snow where the
sleet don't fall and the wind don't blow, In the Big Rock Can- dy
Moun-tain, Oh the buz-zing of the bees in the cig-a-rettes trees, By the
so-da wa-ter foun-tain, By the lem-on-ade springs where the

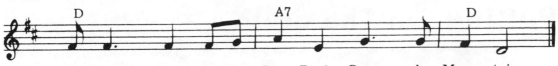

blue-bird   sings, In the   Big   Rock   Can - dy   Moun- tain.

In the Big Rock Candy Mountains you
    never change your socks,
Little streams of alky-hol comes
    trickling down the rocks.
Oh the shacks all have to tip their
    hats and the railroad bulls are
    blind
There's a lake of stew
And gingerale too
And you can paddle all around it
In a big Canoe
In the Big Rock Candy Mountain. (Cho.)

In the Big Rock Candy Mountains the
    cops have wooden legs,
The bull-dogs all have rubber teeth
    and the hens lay soft-boiled eggs.
The Box-cars all are empty and the
    sun shines every day.

I'm bound to go
Where there ain't no snow
Where the sleet don't fall
And the wind don't blow
In the Big Rock Candy Mountain. (Cho.)

In the Big Rock Candy Mountains the
    jails are made of tin,
You can slip right out again as soon as
    they put you in.
There ain't no short handled shovels,
    no axes, saws nor picks.
I'm bound to stay
Where you sleep all day
Where they hung the jerk
That invented work
In the Big Rock Candy Mountain. (Cho.)

Cumberland Gap

(An historic location, where some of the first
colonial pioneers crossed the mountains,
Cumberland Gap is at the south-western tip of
Virginia, bordering Kentucky and Tennessee.)

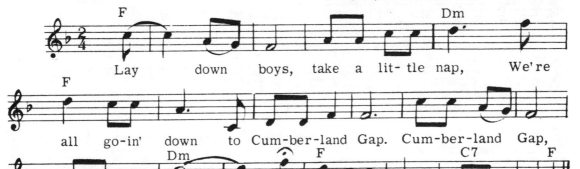

Lay   down   boys, take   a   lit - tle   nap,   We're

all   go-in'   down   to   Cum-ber-land Gap.   Cum-ber-land   Gap,

Cum-ber-land   Gap _____   We're   all go-in' down to Cum-ber-land Gap.

Me and my wife, and my wife's pap
We all live down to Cumberland Gap.
Cumberland Gap, Cumberland Gap
We all live down to Cumberland Gap.

I got a gal in Cumberland Gap,
She's got a baby calls me pap.
Cumberland Gap, Cumberland Gap
We're all goin down to Cumberland Gap.

Cumberland Gap it aint very fur,
It's just three miles from Middlesboro
Cumberland Gap, Cumberland Gap
We're all goin down to Cumberland Gap.

Putting On The Style

(The 1880's, when this song was first sung, was an era of tight corsets for ladies, and the phrase was current: "Let's take the agony out of putting on the style." This version was collected by Norman Cazden and adapted by him from the singing of Ernie Sager, a neighbor of Camp Woodland, in the Catskill Mountains of New York State. The last two verses, typical 1960 additions, are by Jerry Walters of San Francisco.)

(See page 4 for acknowledgement of printed source.)

Young man in a car-riage, driv-ing like he's mad, with a pair of hors-es he bor-rowed from his dad. He cracks his whip so live-ly just to see his la-dy smile, but she knows he's on-ly put-ting on the style.

Chorus

Put-ting on the ag-on-y, put-ting on the style, that's what all the young folks are do-ing all the while. And as I look a- round me, I'm ver-y apt to smile, to see so man-y peo-ple put-ting on the style.

Sweet sixteen goes to Church
Just to see the boys;
Laughs and giggles
At every little noise.
She turns this way a little,
Then turns that way a while,
But everybody knows she's only
Putting on the style.

Young man in a restaurant
Smokes a dirty pipe;
Looking like a pumpkin
That's only half-way ripe.
Smoking, drinking, chewing —
And thinking all the while
That there is nothing equal
To putting on the style.

Young man just from college
Makes a big display
With a great big jawbreak
Which he can hardly say;
It can't be found in Webster's
And won't be for a while,
But everybody knows he's only
Putting on the style.

Preacher in the pulpit
Shouting with all his might,
Glory Hallelujah —
Puts the people in a fright.
You might think that Satan's
Coming up and down the aisle,
But it's only the preacher
Putting on the style.

See the young executive
In his charcoal gray,
Talking with some union men
Who've come to have their say.
Sitting at his office desk
And wearing a toothpaste smile,
That's the executive
Putting on the style.

Congressman from Washington
Looking mighty slick,
Wants to get elected
And go back there right quick.
Beats his breast and hollers
And waves the flag a while,
But we know he's only
Putting on the style.

Rye Whiskey

(A famous late-at-night howler.)

(See page 4 for acknowledgement of printed source.)

Refrain D

Rye whis-key, rye whis-key, rye whis-key I cry. If you

G   D

don't give me rye whis-key, I sure-ly will die.

If the ocean was whiskey and I was a
  duck,
I'd dive to the bottom and never come
  up.

Way up on Clinch Mountain I wander
  alone,
I'm drunk as the devil. Just leave
  me alone.

I'll eat when I'm hungry, I'll drink
  when I'm dry,
If a tree don't fall on me, I'll live
  till I die.

It's whiskey, Rye whiskey, you're
  no friend to me,
You killed my poor daddy,
  Goddam you try me.

Devilish Mary

(Learned from Bess Lomax Hawes, who can sing more songs, and prettier, than any person I know.)

(See page 4 for acknowledgement of printed source.)

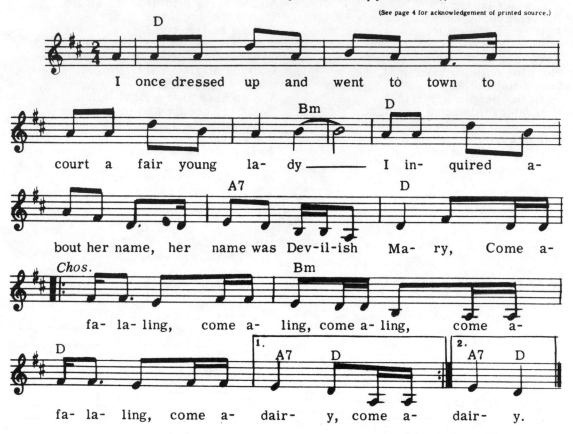

I once dressed up and went to town to court a fair young la- dy ——— I in- quired a- bout her name, her name was Dev- il- ish Ma- ry, Come a-

Chos.
fa- la- ling, come a- ling, come a- ling, come a- fa- la- ling, come a- dair- y, come a- dair- y.

Me and Mary began to spark
She got all in a hurry,
She made it up all in her mind
She'd marry the very next Thursday.
(cho.)

We had not been married for about
two weeks
Before we ought to been parted;
I hadn't said but a single word
She kicked up her heels and started.
(cho.)

She washed my clothes in old soap
suds
She filled my bath with switches
She let me know right at the start
She was going to wear my britches.
(cho.)

Now if I ever marry again
It'll be for love not riches,
Marry a little girl 'bout two feet high
So she can't wear my britches. (cho.)

Yankee Doodle

(History: The song was made up to poke fun at us. We adopted it and made it our own. The tune, of course, is ancient. Dutch, perhaps. "Macaroni" was a term current then for decoration on a uniform — in World War II we called it "scrambled eggs.")

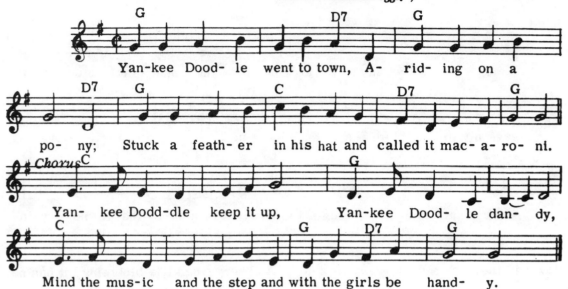

Yan-kee Dood- le went to town, A- rid- ing on a

po- ny; Stuck a feath- er in his hat and called it mac- a- ro- ni.

Chorus

Yan- kee Dodd-dle keep it up, Yan-kee Dood- le dan- dy,

Mind the mus-ic and the step and with the girls be hand- y.

Father and I went down to camp
Along with Captain Gooding;
And there we saw the men and boys,
As thick as hasty pudding.   (Cho.)

There was Captain Washington,
Upon a slapping stallion,
A-giving orders to his men,
I guess there was a million.   (Cho.)

And there we saw a thousand men,
As rich as 'Squire David;
And what they wasted every day,
I wish it could be sa-ved.   (Cho.)

And there I saw a pumpkin shell,
As big as mother's basin,
And every time they touched it off,
They scamper'd like the nation. (Cho.)

Macaroni and Lady, in dress of 1770-75.

mac-a-ro-ni (mak-ạ-rō′-ni), *n.*; pl. *-nis* or *-nies* (-niz). [It. *maccaroni*, now *maccheroni*, pl. of *maccarone*, now *macche-rone*; origin uncertain: cf. *macaroon*.] A kind of paste of Italian origin, prepared from wheat flour, in the form of dried, hollow tubes, to be cooked for food (cf. *spaghetti* and *vermicelli*); also, one of a class of English exquisites or dandies of the 18th century who affected foreign ways (see cut in next column); hence, in general, a

Riddle Song

(I first heard this sung by Burl Ives, in 1938. Can't say where he got it.)

I gave my love a cher-ry that had no stone; I gave my love a chick-en that had no bone; I told my love a sto-ry that had no end; I gave my love a ba-by that's no cry-in'

How can there be a cherry that has no
    stone?
How can there be a chicken that has
    no bone?
How can there be a story that has no
    end?
How can there be a baby that's no
    crying?

A cherry when it's blooming, it has no
    stone,
A chicken when it's pippin' it has no
    bone;
The story that I love you, it has no
    end,
A baby when it's sleeping, it's no
    crying.

Darlin' Corey

(This must have been one of Kentucky's most popular songs in prohibition days — and earlier. I've never met an old time banjo picker in the south who didn't count it one of his favorites.)

Wake up, wake up— dar-lin' Cor-ey, _____ what makes you sleep so sound? The re-ve-nue of- fi- cers are com-in', _____ gon-na tear your still house down. _____

Go 'way, go 'way darlin' Corey,
Quit hangin' around my bed,
Pretty women run me distracted,
Corn liquor's killed me most dead.

Oh yes, oh yes my darlin',
I'll do the best I can,
But I'll never give my pleasure,
To another gamblin' man.

The first time I saw darlin' Corey,
She was standing on the banks of the
    sea,
She had a pistol strapped around her
    body,
And a banjo on her knee.

The last time I saw darlin' Corey,
She had a dram glass in her hand,
She was drinkin' down her troubles,
With a low down gamblin' man.

Dig a hole, dig a hole in the meadow,
Dig a hole in the cold, cold ground,
Go and dig me a hole in the meadow,
Just to lay darlin' Corey down.

Don't you hear them blue-birds
    singing'?
Don't you hear that mournful sound?
They're preachin' Corey's funeral,
In the lonesome graveyard ground.

New River Train

(Don't treat this song too gently; tear up the floor with it, and see how much fun it is.)

1. I'm riding on that new river train, I'm riding on that new river train, It's the same old train that brought me here, It's soon gonna carry me away. 2. Oh darling you can't love but one, Oh darling you can't love but one, Oh you can't love but one and have any fun, oh, darling you can't love but one.

Darling, you can't love two   (2)
You can't love two, and still to me be true.

Darling you can't love three   (2)
You can't love three, and still be true to me.

Darling, you can't love four,   (2)
You can't love four, and love me any more.

Darling, you can't love five   (2)
You can't love five, get your honey from my bee hive.

Darling, you can't love six   (2)
You can't love six, and do any tricks.

Oh, darling you can't love seven   (2)
You can't love seven and expect to get to heaven.

Darling, you can't love eight   (2)
You can't love eight, and get through the Pearly Gates.

Oh, darling you can't love nine,   (2)
You can't love nine, and still be mine.

Repeat first verse

Michael , Row The Boat Ashore*

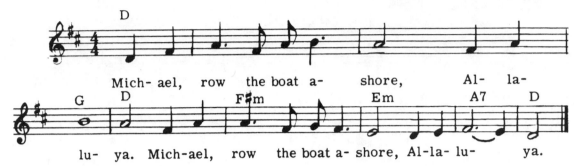

Mich- ael, row the boat a- shore, Al- la- lu- ya. Mich- ael, row the boat a- shore, Al-la- lu- ya.

Michael's boat is a music boat,
   Allaluya,
Michael's boat is a music boat,
   Allaluya.

Michael, row the boat ashore, etc.

Sister help to trim the sail,
   Allaluya,
Sister help to trim the sail,
   Allaluya.

Michael, row the boat ashore, etc.

Jordan's River is deep and wide,
   Allaluya,
Meet my mother on the other side,
   Allaluya.

Michael, row the boat ashore, etc.

Jordan's River is chilly and cold,
   Allaluya,
Kills the body but not the soul,
   Allaluya.

Michael, row the boat ashore, etc.

*Traditional African American song
from Southeastern U.S., mid-19th
Century.

Deep Blue Sea

(Like many an American song, this seems to have been built out of a fragment of an old British ballad or sea song.)

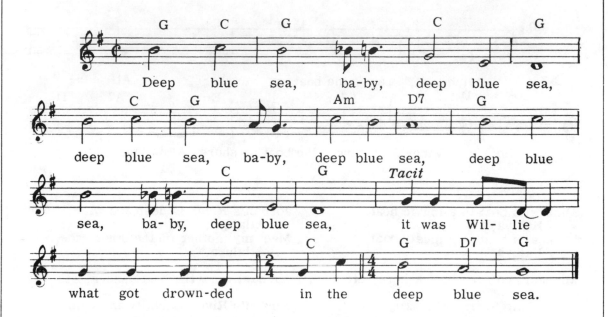

Deep blue sea, ba-by, deep blue sea, deep blue sea, ba-by, deep blue sea, deep blue sea, ba-by, deep blue sea, it was Wil-lie what got drown-ded in the deep blue sea.

Lower him down with a golden chain. (3)
It was Willie what got drownded in the deep blue sea.

Dig his grave with a silver spade. (3)
It was Willie what got drownded in the deep blue sea.

Wrap him up in a silken shroud. (3)
It was Willie what got drownded in the deep blue sea.

Golden sun bring him back to me. (3)
It was Willie what got drownded in the deep blue sea.

IN THE WHALE'S JAWS.

The Water Is Wide

(Another song from England, collected by Cecil Sharp many years ago and titled by him "Waillie, Waillie.")

(See page 4 for acknowledgement of printed source.)

Very Freely

The wat-er is wide, I can-not get o-ver, and nei-ther have I wings to fly. ___ Give me a boat that can car-ry two, ___ And both shall row, ___ My love and I. ___

A ship there is and she sails the sea,
She's loaded deep as deep can be.
But not so deep as the love I'm in,
And I know not how I sink or swim.

I leaned my back up against some
    young oak,
Thinking he was a trusty tree.
But first he bended, and then he broke,
And thus did my false love to me.

I put my hand into some soft bush,
Thinking the sweetest flower to find.
I pricked my finger to the bone,
And left the sweetest flower alone.

Oh, love is handsome and love is fine,
Gay as a jewel when first it is new,
But love grows old, and waxes cold,
And fades away like summer dew.

(Repeat first verse)

Oh, Mary Don't You Weep

(In times of doubt and fear, when threat of atomic war hangs over our heads, this old spiritual has become almost my favorite song.)

If I could I sure-ly would, stand on the rock where
Mo-ses stood. Pha-roah's ar - my got drown-ded
Oh, Ma-ry don't you weep. Oh, Ma- ry don't you
weep don't you mourn, Oh, Ma-ry don't you weep don't you mourn
Pha-roah's ar- my got drown-ded, Oh, Ma- ry don't you weep.

Mary wore three links of chain,
Every link was Jesus name.
Pharoah's army got drownded
Oh, Mary don't you weep.   (Cho.)

Mary wore three links of chain,
Every link was Freedom's name.
Pharoah's army got drownded
Oh, Mary don't you weep.   (Cho.)

One of these nights about twelve
    o'clock,
This old world is gonna reel and rock.
Pharoah's army got drownded
Oh, Mary don't you weep.   (Cho.)

Moses stood on the Red Sea shore,
Smotin' the water with a two-by-four.
Pharoah's army got drownded
Oh, Mary don't you weep.   (Cho.)

God gave Noah the rainbow sign,
No more water but fire next time.
Pharoah's army got drownded
Oh, Mary don't you weep.   (Cho.)

The Lord told Moses what to do,
To lead those Hebrew children through.
Pharoah's army got drownded
Oh, Mary don't you weep.   (Cho.)

Barbara Allen

(Samuel Pepys wrote in his 17th Century diary: "Heard this evening the delightful new Scottish song, Barbara Ellen." Probably it is the most widespread old world ballad in the U.S. — of course, everyone knows a different version and swears it is "the real one.")

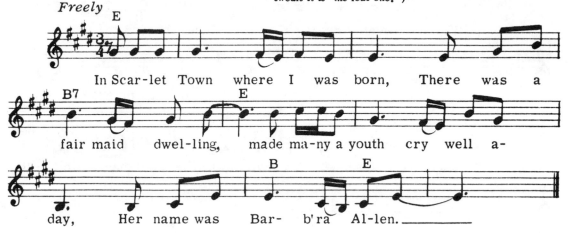

Freely

In Scar-let Town where I was born, There was a fair maid dwel-ling, made ma-ny a youth cry well a-day, Her name was Bar- b'ra Al-len._____

It was in the merry month of May
When green buds they were swelling;
Sweet William came from the west
   country
And he courted Barbara Allen.

He sent his servant unto her
To the place where she was dwelling;
Said my master's sick, bids me call
   for you
If your name be Barbara Allen.

Well, slowly, slowly got she up
And slowly went she nigh him;
But all she said as she passed his bed
Young man I think you're dying.

Then lightly tripped she down the stairs
She heard those church bells tolling;
And each bell seemed to say as it tolled
Hard-hearted Barbara Allen.

O, mother, mother go make my bed
And make it long and narrow;
Sweet William died for me today
I'll die for him tomorrow.

They buried Barbara in the old church
   yard
They buried Sweet William beside her;
Out of his grave grew a red, red rose
And out of hers a briar.

They grew and grew up the old church
   wall
Till they could grow no higher;
And at the top twined in a lovers' knot
The red rose and the briar.

The Fox

(It's nice to find the fox for once treated as the hero.)

The fox went out on a chil-ly night, Prayed for the moon to give him light, For he'd ma-ny a mile to go that night be-fore he reached the town- o, town-o, town - o, he'd ma-ny a mile to go that night be - fore he reached the town - o.

He ran till he came to a great big bin
The ducks and the geese were put
   therein,
Said, a couple of you will grease my
   chin
Before I leave this town-o, etc.

He grabbed the grey goose by the neck
Slung the little one over his back,
He didn't mind their quack-quack-
   quack
And the legs all dangling down-o, etc.

Old mother pitter-patter jumped out of
   bed
Out of the window she cocked her head
Crying, John, John, the grey goose is
   gone
And the fox is on the town-o, etc.

John, he went to the top of the hill
Blew his horn both loud and shrill;
The fox, he said, I better flee with my
   kill
He'll soon be on my trail-o, etc.

He ran till he came to his cozy den
There were the little ones, eight, nine,,
   ten,
They said daddy, you better go back
   again,
'Cause it must be a mighty fine town-
   o, etc.

Then the fox and his wife without any
   strife
Cut up the goose with fork and knife,
They never had such a supper in their
   life
And the little ones chewed on the
   bones-o, etc.

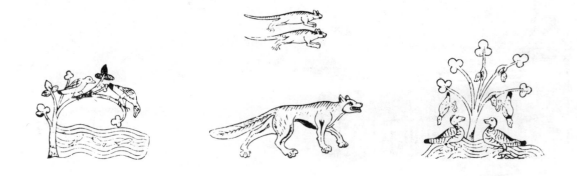

Twelve Gates To The City

Oh, what a beau-ti-ful ci-ty; Oh, what a
beau-ti-ful ci-ty; Oh, what a beau-ti-ful ci-ty,
twelve gates to the ci-ty, hal-le-loo____ yah!

1. Three gates in the East; three gates in the West; three gates in the North;
three gates in the South; there's twelve gates to the ci-ty, hal-le-loo-
yah!

2. Who are those child-ren there
It must be the child-ren that

dressed in red? There's twelve gates to the
Mo-ses led, There's twelve gates to the
ci-ty, hal-le-loo____ yah,
ci-ty, hal-le-loo_____ yah!

My God done just what He said,
There's twelve gates (etc.)
He healed the sick and He raised
 the dead,
There's twelve gates (etc.) (cho.)

Only one thing that we did wrong,
There's, etc.
Was staying in the wilderness too long,
There's, etc.

When I get to heaven, going to sing
 and shout,
There's twelve gates (etc.)
Ain't nobody there going to put me out,
There's twelve gates (etc.) (cho.)

Three gates in the east!
Three gates in the west!
Three gates in the north!
Three gates in the south!
There's, etc.

John Henry

(The noblest American ballad of them all. I first heard it
played on the harmonica by painter Tom Benton. The older
I grow, the more facets of meaning I see in the story. It,
too, can be traced to historical fact, in West Virginia's
Swannanoa Tunnel in the 1880's, I'm told. But the song was
just born then. Now it's grown.)

When John Hen-ry was a lit-tle ba—by,

sit-ting on his pa—pa's knee, Well he picked up a ham-mer and a

lit-tle piece of steel, said "ham-mer's gon-na be the death of

me Lord, Lord: Ham-mer's gon-na be the death of me."

The captain said to John Henry,
"I'm gonna bring that steam drill
    around,
I'm gonna bring that steam drill out on
    the job,
I'm gonna whup that steel on down."
    (Lord, Lord!) (4)

John Henry told his captain,
"Lord a man ain't nothing but a man,
But before I'd let your steam drill
    beat me down,
I'd die with a hammer in my hand! "
    (Lord, Lord) (4)

John Henry said to his shaker,
"Shaker why don't you sing?
Because I'm swinging thirty pounds
    from my hips on down;
Just listen to that cold steel ring."
    (Lord, Lord) (4)

Now the captain said to John Henry,
"I believe that mountain's caving in."
John Henry said right back to the
    captain,
"Ain't nothing but my hammer sucking
    wind." (Lord, Lord) (4)

Now the man that invented the steam
    drill,
He thought he was mighty fine;
But John Henry drove fifteen feet,
The steam drill only made nine.
    (Lord, Lord) (4)

John Henry hammered in the mountains,
His hammer was striking fire,
But he worked so hard, it broke his poor
    poor heart
And he laid down his hammer and he
    died. (Lord, Lord) (4)

Now John Henry had a little woman,
Her name was Polly Anne,
John Henry took sick and had to go to
    bed,
Polly Anne drove steel like a man.
    (Lord, Lord) (4)

John Henry had a little baby,
You could hold him in the palm of your
    hand;
And the last words I heard that poor
    boy say,
"My daddy was a steel driving man."
    (Lord, Lord) (4)

So every Monday morning
When the blue birds begin to sing,
You can hear John Henry a mile or
    more;
You can hear John Henry's hammer
    ring. (Lord, Lord) (4)

NAT TURNER,

Swanee River

(Stephen Foster's sentimental songs were typical of mid-19th
Century America. But shorn of their minstrel show dialect
and considered simply as melodies, it is no wonder they
spread around the world. He had a genius for fitting
syllables to tunes.)

Way down u-pon the Swa-nee ri-ver, far far a-way,

There's where my heart is turn-ing e-ver, That's where the old folks

stay. All the world is sad and drear-y, Ev'-ry where I roam.

Old broth-er how my heart grows wear-y, Far from the old folks at home.

All up and down the whole creation,
    Sadly I roam,
Still longing for the old plantation,
    And for the old folks at home.
                            (Cho.)

All round the little farm I wandered,
    When I was young.
Then many happy days I squandered,
    Many the songs I sung.   (Cho.)

One little hut among the bushes,
    One that I love;
Still sadly to my memory rushes,
    No matter where I rove.   (Cho.)

When will I see the bees a-humming,
    All round the comb?
When will I hear the banjos strumming
    Down in my good old home? (Cho.)

Reuben James

SUNKEN DESTROYER
AN OLD 4-STACKER

(Written by Woody Guthrie and the Almanac Singers in November, 1941.)

(See page 4 for acknowledgement of printed source.)

Narrative Style

Have you heard of the ship called the good Reu-ben

James, Mann'd by hard fight-ing men both of hon- or and fame? She

flew the Stars and Stripes of the Land of the Free, But to-

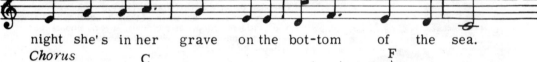

night she's in her grave on the bot-tom of the sea.

Chorus

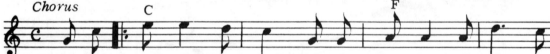

Tell me, what were their names, Tell me, what were their names? Did

you have a friend on the good Reu-ben James? good Reu-ben James?

It was there in the dark of that
   uncertain night,
That we watched for the U-boats,
   and waited for the fight.
Then the fire, and the rock, and
   the great explosion roared,
They laid the Reuben James
   on the cold ocean floor. (Cho.)

Now tonight there are lights in our
   country so bright,
In the farms and in the cities, they're
   telling of the fight,
And now our mighty battleships will
   steam the bounding main,
And remember the name of that
   good Reuben James. (Cho.)

REUBEN JAMES HIT

First American Warship
Lost in War Torpedoed
West of Iceland

The Wabash Cannon Ball

(Another hobo song in origin. The words, half of which must be incomprehensible to most people, have a wild rush of imagery.)

I stood on the At-lan-tic o-cean, On the wide Pa- ci- fic shore, Heard the Queen of flow-ing moun-tains to the South Belle by the door. She's long, tall and hand-some, she's loved by one and all. She's a mod-ern com-bin- a- tion called the Wa-bash Can- non- ball.

Chos

Lis-ten to the jin-gle, The rum-ble and the roar. Rid-ing thru the wood-lands, to the hill and by the shore. Hear the might-y rush of en-gines, Hear the lone-some ho-bo squall, Rid-ing thru the jun-gles on the Wa- bash Can- non – ball.

Now the eastern states are dandies, so
   the western people say
From New York to St. Louis and
   Chicago by the way,
Thru the hills of Minnesota where the
   rippling waters fall
No chances can be taken on the
   Wabash Cannonball.   (Cho.)

Here's to Daddy Claxton, may his
   name forever stand
Will he be remembered through parts
   of all our land,
When his earthly race is over and the
   curtain round him falls
We'll carry him on to victory on the
   Wabash Cannonball.   (Cho.)

Crawdad

(The crawdad, or crawfish, looks like a miniature (3 - 5 inch) lobster, lives in brooks, and can be eaten. But of course that's not what the song is all about anyway.)

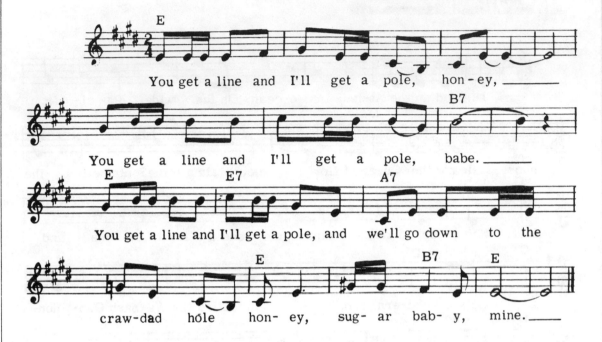

You get a line and I'll get a pole, hon-ey, _____
You get a line and I'll get a pole, babe. _____
You get a line and I'll get a pole, and we'll go down to the
craw-dad hole hon-ey, sug-ar bab-y, mine. _____

Get up old man, you slept too late,
  honey, (2)
Get up old man, you slept too late,
Last piece of crawdad's on your plate,
Honey, sugar-baby mine.

Get up old woman, you slept too late,
  honey, (2)
Get up old woman, you slept too late,
Crawdad man done passed your gate,
Honey, sugar-baby mine.

Along come a man with a sack on his
  back, honey, (2)
Along come a man with a sack on his
  back,
Packin' all the crawdads he can pack,
Honey, sugar-baby mine.

What you gonna do when the lake goes
  dry, honey? (2)
What you gonna do when the lake goes
  dry,
Sit on the bank and watch the crawdads
  die,
Honey, sugar-baby mine.

What you gonna do when the crawdads
  die, honey? (2)
What you gonna do when the crawdads
  die,
Sit on the bank until I cry,
Honey, sugar-baby mine.

I heard the duck say to the drake,
  honey, (2)
I heard the duck say to the drake,
There ain't no crawdads in this lake,
Honey, sugar-baby mine.

Erie Canal

(New York State's finest claim to fame, this song is a classic
of the old canal days, with mules towing the barges through.
It has a hundred verses, ribald and rowdy, and may we all
be as light hearted as the fellows who first sang it.)

We were for-ty miles from Al- ban- y forget it, I nev-er shall. What a ter-rib- le storm we
had one night, on the E- ri- e Can- al. Oh the E-ri-e was a
ris- ing, And the gin was a get-ting low. And I scarce-ly think we'll
get a drink, till we get to Buf-fa-lo,—Till we get to Buf- fa- lo.

We were loaded down with barley,	The cook she was a grand old gal,
We were chock-up full on rye;	She wore a ragged dress,
The captain he looked down on me	We heisted her upon the pole
With his gol-durn wicked eye. (Cho.)	As a signal of distress. (Cho.)
Two days out from Syracuse,	The wind begin to whistle,
The vessel struck a shoal,	The waves begin to roll,
We like to all be foundered	We had to reef our royals
On a chunk o' Lackawanna coal. (Cho.)	On that raging Canal. (Cho.)
We hollered to the captain	When we got to Syracuse,
On the towpath, treadin' dirt,	Off-mule he was dead,
He jumped on board and stopped the leak	The nigh mule he got blind staggers
With his old red flannel shirt. (Cho.)	We cracked him on the head. (Cho.)

The captain, he got married,
The cook, she went to jail,
And I'm the only sea-cook son
That's left to tell the tale. (Cho.)

Dink's Song

(In 1908 John Lomax listened to a woman sing as she washed clothes for her man working in a levee camp. Next year he tried to look her up again. The townspeople motioned up to the end of the street where the graveyard was. "That's where Dink's living now." The Lomax family remembered her song and passed it on to us, a great flower of beauty.)

(See page 4 for acknowledgement of printed source.)

If I had wings like No- ah's dove, I'd fly 'cross the ri-ver to the man I love. Fare thee well Oh, hon-ey fare thee well.

That gal I love, she's long and tall.
She moves her body like a cannonball.
   Fare thee well, etc.

One of these days, and it won't be long,
You call my name, and I'll be gone.
   Fare thee well, etc.

When I wore my apron low,
Couldn't keep you from my door.
   Fare thee well, etc.

Now I wear my apron high,
Scarcely ever see you passing by.
   Fare thee well, etc.

One of these night, was a drizzling rain,
All around my heart was an aching pain.
   Fare thee well, etc.

If I had wings, like Noah's dove,
I'd fly up the river, to the one I love.
   Fare thee well, etc.

Hard Traveling

(Words and music by Woody Guthrie. Give it a steady, hard beat, and it will give out that hard-times, hard working feeling.)

(See page 4 for acknowledgement of printed source.)

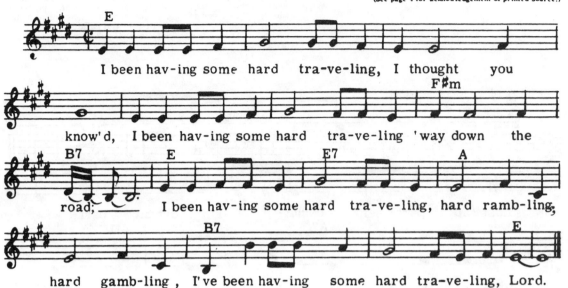

I been hav-ing some hard tra-ve-ling, I thought you know'd, I been hav-ing some hard tra-ve-ling 'way down the road;___ I been hav-ing some hard tra-ve-ling, hard ramb-ling, hard gamb-ling, I've been hav-ing some hard tra-ve-ling, Lord.

I been doing some hard harvesting
    I thought you know'd
I been working the Kansas wheat
    fields 'way down the road;
Cutting that wheat and stacking that
    hay, trying to make 'bout a dollar
    a day
I been having some hard traveling,
    Lord.

I been a riding them fast rattlers,
    I thought you know'd
I been a riding them flat wheelers
    Way down the road;
I been a riding them blind passengers,
    Dead enders, kickin' up cinders,
I been having some hard traveling,
    Lord.

I've been working in a hard-rock
    tunnel I thought you know'd
I been leaning on a pressure drill
    'way down the road;
Hammer flying, airhose sucking, six
    feet of mud and I sure been a-
    mucking
I been having some hard traveling,
    Lord.

I been a layin' in a hard rock jail
    I thought you know'd
I been a layin' out ninety days
    Way down the road;
Mean old judge he says to me
    It's ninety days for vagrancy
I been having some hard traveling,
    Lord.

Skip To My Lou

(Young people in many a 19th midwestern community were not allowed to dance. It was sinful, said the adults. The youths asked, "Is it all right if we play some games?" Thus evolved the American invention known as the play party: a square dance or ring dance accompanied not by instruments, but by handclapping and singing — and called a "play party," NOT a dance. "Skip to my Lou" was always a favorite.)

Lost my part- ner what -'ll I do,

Lost my part- ner, what-'ll I do, Lost my part- ner,

what-'ll I do? Skip to my Lou my dar- ling.

Chorus:
Gone again, skip to my Lou
Gone again, skip to my Lou
Gone again, skip to my Lou
Skip to my Lou my darling.

Little red wagon painted blue
Little red wagon painted blue
Little red wagon painted blue
Skip to my Lou my darling. (Cho.)

I'll get another one prettier than you
I'll get another one prettier than you
I'll get another one prettier than you
Skip to my Lou my darling. (Cho.)

Flies in the buttermilk two by two
Flies in the buttermilk two by two
Flies in the buttermilk two by two
Skip to my Lou my darling.   (Cho.)

Flies in the sugar bowl shoo shoo shoo, etc.

Going to Texas two by two, etc.

Cat's in the cream jar what'll I do?, etc.

(See how many more verses you can recollect or invent)

Solidarity Forever

(As we sing songs of past centuries, wars, and revolutions, to remind us of the struggles which our forefathers have undertaken perhaps it is time we also recognize other pioneers, condemned by many in their day, but whose work perhaps helped us all. The words are by Ralph Chaplin of the I.W.W., half a century ago.)

Chorus

Sol- i- dar- i- ty for ev- er, Sol- i- dar- i- ty for- ev- er, Sol- i- dar- i- ty for- ev- er, for the Un- ion makes us strong.

When the Un- ion's in-spir- a- tion thru the work- ers' blood shall run, There can be no pow- er great- er an- y where be- neath the sun; Yet what force on earth is weak- er than the feeb- le strength of one, For the Un- ion makes us strong.

It is we who plowed the prairies, built
   the cities where they trade,
Dug the mines and built the workshops,
   endless miles of railroad laid,
Now we stand, outcast and starving,
   mid the wonders we have made
But the union makes us strong. (Cho.)

They have taken untold millions that
   they never toiled to earn,
But without our brain and muscle not
   a single wheel can turn,
We can break their haughty power,
   gain our freedom when we learn
That the union makes us strong.(Cho.)

In our hands is placed a power greater
   than their hoarded gold,
Greater than the might of atoms,*
   magnified a thousandfold,
We can bring to birth a new world
   from the ashes of the old
For the union makes us strong. (Cho.)

* Originally "armies"

So Long,
It's Been Good To Know You

(Woody Guthrie first became famous in the 1930's as the composer of a series of ballads of the Oklahoma dust storms and the trek to California. This song is destined to be sung by many millions who never otherwise heard of a dust storm.)

(See page 4 for acknowledgement of printed source.)

I've sung this song but I'll sing it a-gain of the place that I lived on the wild wind-y plain, In the month of A-pril, the coun-ty called Gray Here's what all of the peo-ple there say! Well it's

Chorus

So long, it's been good to know you, So long, it's been good to know you, So long, it's been good to know you, This dust-y old dust is a get-ting my home and I've got to be drift-ing a-long.

Well the dust storm came, it came
   like thunder
It dusted us over, it covered us under
It blocked out the traffic, it blocked
   out the sun
And straight for home all the people
   did run.   (Cho.)

Well the sweethearts they sat in the
   dark and they sparked
They hugged and they kissed in that
   dusty old dark;
They sighed, they cried, they hugged
   and they kissed
But instead of marriage, they were
   talking like this, honey   (Cho.)

Now the telephone rang and it jumped
    off the wall
That was the preacher, he was a-
    making his call.
He said, "Kind friends this may be
    the end
You've got your last chance at salva-
    tion of sin." (No chorus here)

Well the churches were jammed, the
    churches were packed
That dusty old dust-storm it blew so
    black
The preacher could not read a word of
    his text
He folded his specs —— took up
    collection, said   (Cho.)

Kisses Sweeter Than Wine

(A classic example of how American songs have been put
together; the original tune was Irish — a free, wandering
melody in a minor mode. Leadbelly liked it, but wanted
to play it in his own way — he added rhythm. Later, I
thought of a new set of words for the chorus. Lee Hays
wrote a dozen verses and the rest of The Weavers helped
pare them down to a usable five.)

(See page 4 for acknowledgement of printed source.)

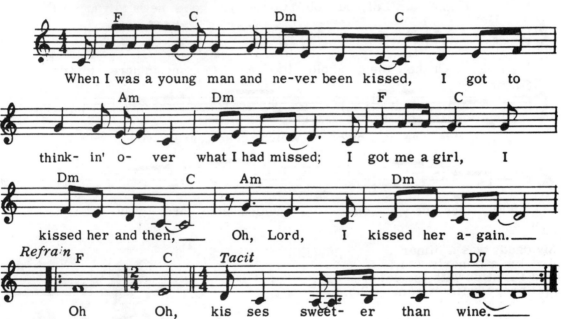

When I was a young man and ne-ver been kissed, I got to
think-in' o-ver what I had missed; I got me a girl, I
kissed her and then,___ Oh, Lord, I kissed her a-gain.___

Refrain
Oh   Oh, kis ses sweet-er than wine.___

He asked me to marry and be his sweet
    wife,
And we would be so happy the rest of
    our life.
He begged and he pleaded like a natural
    man,
And then, oh, Lord, I gave him my
    hand.   (Refrain)

I worked mighty hard and so did my
    wife,
A-workin' hand in hand to make a good
    life.
With corn in the fields and wheat in the
    bins,
And then, oh, Lord, I was the father
    of twins.   (Refrain)

Our children numbered just about four,
And they all had sweethearts knocking
    at the door.
They all got married and they didn't
    hesitate,
I was, oh, Lord, the grandfather
    (mother) of eight.   (Refrain)

Now we are old and ready to go,
We get to thinkin' what happened a
    long time ago,
We had a lot of kids, trouble and pain,
But, oh, Lord, we'd do it again.
    (Refrain)

Which Side Are You On?

(Mrs. Florence Reece, wife of a rank and file organizer for the old National Miner's Union in Harlan County, Kentucky, 1931, was at home one day when the High Sheriff J. H. Blair and his "deputies" ("they were really company gun thugs" she related) came to her house. One of her little girls started to cry. "What you crying for?" said a deputy. "We ain't after you; we're after your old man." They poked their rifles into closets, under beds, even into piles of dirty clothes, and finally left. Mrs. Reece tore an old calendar off the wall and wrote these now famous verses. She fitted it to an old hymn tune, and her little girls used to sing it at the union hall.)

(See page 4 for acknowledgement of printed source.)

Come all of you good work- ers, good news to you I'll tell Of how the good old Un-ion has come in here to dwell.

Chorus

Which side are you on? Which side are you on?

Which side are you on? Which side are you on?

My daddy was a miner
And I'm a miner's son,*
And I'll stick with the union
'Til every battle's won. (Cho.)

They say in Harlan County
There are no neutrals there;
You'll either be a union man
Or a thug for J.H. Blair. (Cho.)

Oh workers can you stand it?
Oh tell me how you can.
Will you be a lousy scab
Or will you be a man? (Cho.)

Don't scab for the bosses,
Don't listen to their lies.
Us poor folks haven't got a chance
Unless we organize. (Cho.)

* Originally as sung by Mrs. Reece's daughters: "He's now in the air and sun" -- meaning blacklisted from the mines.

A PAGE OF GUITAR CHORDS

Many folk musicians that I know play beautiful accompaniments on the guitar, but only in a few keys, such as E, A, D, G, or C. And if the song is in a minor key they will play it in Em, Am, or Dm. If they need, for any reason, to play a song in any other key, they use a capo; unless you prefer not to, I would really advise you to do the same.

Thus, if you have to play a song in the key of F, simply affix the capo one fret up, and play in E. Where a B♭ chord is called for, sound an A, and where a C7 is needed, just play B7.

If the song is in C minor, affix the capo three frets up, and play in A minor. Where an F minor chord is called for, play D m, and so on.

With this prefatory note, I show below, for reference only, a few of the many hundreds of variations of chords possible on the guitar. Do not try to memorize them, but learn them only when necessary. The success of a chord often depends on which bass note you strike, and which strings you don't sound. A good guitarist is often known not so much by the notes he plays, as by the notes he doesn't play. As brevity is the soul of wit, economy can be the soul of music.

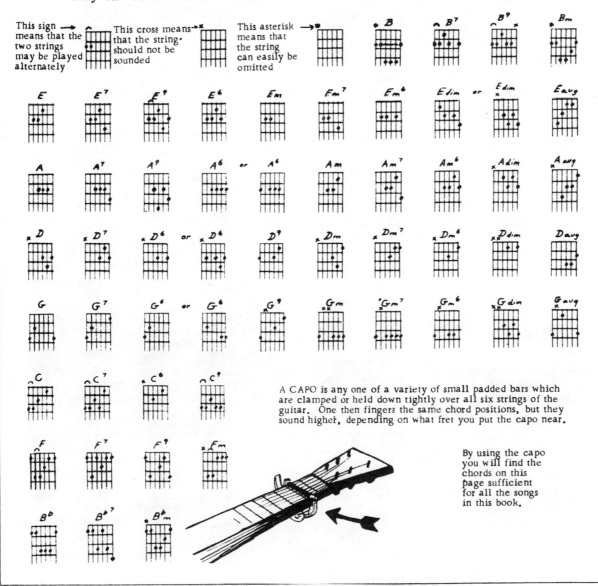

A CAPO is any one of a variety of small padded bars which are clamped or held down tightly over all six strings of the guitar. One then fingers the same chord positions, but they sound higher, depending on what fret you put the capo near.

By using the capo you will find the chords on this page sufficient for all the songs in this book.

Discography

Pete Seeger's renditions of the songs in this book may be heard on Folkways Records. Here is a listing of all the songs in this collection with the appropriate record reference. For more information on the recordings, write to Folkways Records, 701 Seventh Ave., N.Y.C., N.Y. 10036

(*) sung by Woody Guthrie